THE WORLD OF LIZARDS

THE WORLD OF

Lizards

G. Earl Chace

*Illustrated with photographs
by the author*

DODD, MEAD & COMPANY · NEW YORK

1   2   3   4   5   6   7   8   9   10

Library of Congress Cataloging in Publication Data

Chace, G. Earl
    The world of lizards.

Bibliography: p.
    Includes index.
    Summary: Describes the physical characteristics and
life cycle of a variety of lizards, including the monitors, chameleons, and iguanas.
    1. Lizards—Juvenile literature.   I. Title.
QL666.L2C43   597.95   81-19421
ISBN O-396-08043-X   AACR2

I would like to dedicate this book to all my friends and colleagues who have aided me:

To Ray Pawley, Reptile Curator of Brookfield Zoo, Chicago, who courageously read and made some needed corrections;

To Joe Maierhauser, Assistant Manager, and Bill Texel, Curator of the Black Hills Reptile Gardens, who helped me in taking some of the pictures and also in the identification of those taken many years ago;

To Earl Brockelsby, who gave me unlimited use of his library and access to his collection of reptiles at the Black Hills Reptile Gardens;

To Edith, my wife, my critic, my typist, who encouraged me in this endeavor.

CONTENTS

THE WORLD OF LIZARDS

1

INTRODUCING THE LIZARDS

Seeing a lizard dash swiftly across the ground or up a tree can be a thrill but a frustrating one. It's all over too quickly and leaves many questions unanswered. What type of lizard was it? Was it running from you, or after a mouthful of food, and if so, what kind of food? Discovering answers to questions like these was one of the privileges I had as Curator of the Black Hills Reptile Gardens in South Dakota. Under a transparent dome, in a living tropical jungle, lizards live a normal and almost free life, even to eating or being eaten by either bird or snake that shares the area with them. They gradually grow accustomed to visitors who follow a winding path through the open exhibit which allows close observation and photographs to be made.

During my years of sharing the Reptile Gardens with the public and caring for the dome inhabitants, I learned how fascinating lizards can be, far more quickly and more easily than pursuing them in the wilds of the world. Of course, some lizards are too large or too dangerous to be turned loose in such an area, but over the years those that could lived freely and well. They taught those of us who cared for them much about their private lives. And much of what was learned under the dome will be brought out in the following pages.

The lizards are the most abundant form of reptile life found in the world today. There are approximately 3,000 species, which vary considerably in shape, size, color, habits, and habitat. They range from about one and one-half inches to ten feet in length, and from two ounces to three hundred pounds in weight. At least one species can be found on every continent, except Antarctica, and on every major island. They inhabit all environments, from the moist jungles of the equatorial regions to the hot, dry deserts. One species even manages to survive within the Arctic Circle.

The history of lizards began about 300 million years ago when the first lizard evolved from the amphibians. Amphibians are thin-skinned, scaleless, semiaquatic creatures that are bound to the water. Their eggs, which have no shell, must be hatched in water. Their poorly developed lungs cannot obtain sufficient oxygen from the air, so the skin must also absorb oxygen from the surroundings. The skin has to be moist to function; if it becomes dry, the amphibian dies. Amphibians survive today as frogs, toads, and salamanders.

It was from the giant, prehistoric salamander that the lizard evolved. The most important changes from amphibian to reptile were the development of a shell around the egg, a dry, protective skin, and more efficient lungs.

The change from amphibian to reptile did not happen all at once; far from it. The first indication of change was discovered in the fossils that were found in coal beds that were formed approximately 360 millions years ago. Here were found the fossilized remains of many different, but closely related, lizardlike creatures that have been placed in the Order Cotylosauria. This is an arbitrary order that could be classified as either amphibian or reptile. Until proven otherwise by fossils yet to be found, the Cotylosauria will continue to be considered the ancestors of all reptiles and are called the stem reptiles. The first true lizards were found in fossil beds that were formed about 300 million years ago, indicating that it took at least 60 million years to complete the change from amphibians to reptiles.

14

A contemporary salamander. Note the smooth skin and four, clawless toes on each foot.

With a shell-covered egg that could hatch in soil, plus a dry, non-porous, scaly, protective skin, and adequate lungs, the newly evolved reptiles were completely free of the water. They could now invade the land, and were the first of the land animals.

The land areas of the world at that time were well populated with plants and insects, but no mammals or birds. The lizards could therefore go anywhere and find food, with no enemies other than their own kind. As they spread across the land in search of food, they encountered many different environments. The lizards were not all alike.

15

Those with longer claws could best climb trees. Those with longer legs could run faster. The lizards with the most suitable equipment and ability in each new environment were the ones to survive, to dominate their less fortunate relatives, and to reproduce. Each succeeding generation produced young better suited to that area.

The pursuits of food and shelter are the prime reasons for specialization. With all lizards terrestrial and seeking only insects on the ground, competition grew too great. To survive this pressure, some lizards went into the trees and shrubs, others went underground, and a few returned to the water. Some ate only insects, others added mice and eggs to their diet, while many became cannibalistic. A few lizards began an omnivorous diet, which includes about everything from insects to vegetation. Such diversity allowed many lizards to live well in one small area. It also forced, by means of natural selection, a great variety of sizes, colors, and shapes to better cope in their new hunting grounds.

The functions and results of natural selection have already been demonstrated by the changes of the amphibians to lizards and again by diversification of the lizards. The young produced by a male and a female who are well adapted to their environment inherit these favorable characteristics. Thus, they have a better chance to live and reproduce and again pass on these strong characteristics necessary for survival. The weak and unfit gradually die out.

Today, after millions of years of change, there are lizards that feed under saltwater, hide under freshwater, glide or parachute from tall trees, run upside down across household ceilings, climb up smooth panes of glass, spend their lives underground, "swim" through hot desert sands, or even run on top of water. There are also lizards that have lost their hind legs, or all four legs and resemble snakes, and a few underground lizards that resemble earthworms and no longer have eyes. Scales may be smooth, pinecone rough, or elongated into horns, fringes, or spines. Skins may fit snugly or have flaps along the sides,

16

A common iguana, showing dewlap, fringe, tympanum, five toes with claws

webbed toes, fringes about the neck, or merely hang down from the throat as a dewlap.

Despite such variations, there are certain characteristics that lizards must have to be called a lizard. Most species will possess them all but some will lack one or two characteristics and yet retain enough to be a member of the Suborder Lacertilia.

17

Because they are reptiles and belong to the Class Reptilia, all lizards are ectothermic, which means they are cold-blooded. They cannot generate a body temperature as the mammals and birds do, but seek their warmth from their surroundings, such as the rays from the warm sun. Neither do lizards have the benefit of cooling sweat glands; they must seek shelter or shade in times of excessive heat.

Basically, lizards have four legs with five clawed toes on each foot. They are equipped with two eyes and functional eyelids. Some species also have a third, transparent, sideways-moving eyelid on each eye called the nictitating membrane. This membrane is normally found only on lizards that live in areas of gusty winds and blowing sand. By leaving the eyelids open and sliding the transparent nictitating membranes across its eyes, a lizard has both sight and protection during a sandstorm. Lizards also have ear openings seen as holes, slits, or external plates called tympanums.

Due to the fact that many harmless, legless lizards are confused with snakes, and feared or even killed in the belief that they are poisonous snakes, it seems proper to note the distinction. All snakes lack ear openings, visual legs (some species do have internal, vestigial legs), and eyelids. A final check, best performed on dead specimens, is that the lower jaw of the snake is not joined in front by bone. There is no chin, only soft, flexible tissue that connects the jaw. Lizards have a continuous bony lower jaw—in other words, a chin.

Lizards detect odor by means of two glands called Jacobson's organs that open on the upper, inside surface of their mouths, which are lined with the nerves of smell. Some species, such as the monitors, have flicking, forked tongues which transfer odors from the air to these organs. Other species use their nostrils to bring air and odor to the glands.

Most lizards have a third or pineal eye located in the center of the top of the head. It can be seen as a tiny, pearl-colored spot. This eye is apparently a vestigial organ, one that is no longer of any use, since it is not fully developed in a modern-day lizard. Little is known of the pineal eye's use to the ancient lizards because soft tissue, such as eyes, does not fossilize. However, it must be assumed that the third eye did have some value for them.

The top of a Bengal monitor head, showing the pineal eye

Lizards have poor blood circulation because they have a three-valved heart. In a four-valved heart, such as mammals have, blood is pumped into the lungs to be charged with fresh oxygen and relieved of its impurities. Then the pure oxygenated blood is pumped directly through the body to regenerate the muscle tissue. The three-valved heart of the lizard is less efficient. With no fourth valve, the freshly oxygenated blood is mixed with impure blood and then pumped through the body. This does not allow a fast recuperative period from excessive activity. Lizards must spend considerable time in resting or sunning themselves.

Other than the mouth, eyes, nostrils, and ears, the only opening on the body is a vent which is located on the underside of the base of the tail. It is used for reproduction and the ridding of body wastes. It is, in all lizards, a crosswise slit. Although possessing a urinary bladder, many lizards do not urinate. The excess water is reclaimed by glands and a paste of urea is discharged along with the feces.

Mating is more or less similar with all lizards, which were the first animals to practice internal reproduction. All produce eggs, but some species retain the shell-less eggs within the body until the embryo is fully developed and then give birth to active young. Some give birth to mature embryos still enclosed in their transparent amnion sacs from which they immediately struggle. This method is called live-bearing or ovoviviparous. Other lizards, after mating, lay their leathery-shelled eggs in protective places and allow the warmth and

Anolis carolinensis, *the American chameleon*

moisture of rotted grasses or warm, moist soil to hatch them. This is called egg laying or oviparous.

Many species of lizards have a strange method of protecting themselves other than the normal running, hiding, bluffing, or biting. It is called autotomy. These lizards have several breaking points through the center of the tail vertebrae. The muscles and tissues surrounding these areas are also capable of parting. If grasped, especially by the tail, the lizard exerts muscular pressure or pull at one of the breaking points and the tail breaks off clean. The lizard immediately runs away, but the dropped tail remains thrashing and wriggling for some minutes, powered by reflex action. The mobile tail often occupies the enemy long enough to enable the lizard to escape.

Some lizards are widely dispersed and the expression "Old World" and "New World" will be used now and then. The Old World includes Asia, Africa, Australia, and Europe, plus the adjacent islands. The New World refers to North and South America, plus islands.

The lizards have been divided into eighteen families, and the sixteen major ones are covered in the following chapters. The other two families are so uncommon that their members are rarely, if ever, seen. Because of the tremendous variation of the species, some of the lesser-known species may someday be added to, as more is learned, or possibly dropped from existing families. The scientific position of lizards in the Animal Kingdom may be shown by classifying the well-known American chameleon, *Anolis carolinensis*.

Class:	Reptilia (all reptiles)
Order:	Squamata (snakes and lizards)
Suborder:	Lacertilia (lizards)
Family:	Iguanidae
Genus:	*Anolis*
Species:	*carolinensis*

21

2

THE MONITORS

Family Varanidae

An irritated or defensive large monitor lizard can be an awesome sight. It rears high on its legs, points its elongated head this way and that, glares through fierce eyes, and flicks a long, forked tongue in and out. Its heavy, long, powerful, laterally compressed tail slowly moves from side to side as if trying to decide in which direction it should lash out. Its claws dig into the soil as if seizing prey. Now and then its sides bulge out as the lizard inhales air and expels it with a hiss.

All thirty species of monitors are fierce, meat-eating lizards. They are designed for whatever running, climbing, digging, or fighting may be necessary for obtaining their prey. Unlike most lizards, many of the scales on the monitors have small slivers of bone underlying them which serve as a partial armor. Monitors are also unique in having the back portion of the lower jaw capable of unhinging from the skull and swinging down. This enables the monitor to open its mouth far enough to swallow much of its prey whole. Loose skin about the throat stretches to allow such food to pass.

Monitors are tropical reptiles. They are found in Africa, Australia, India, and over much of Asia and the East Indies. They can be found crashing through the open fields of dry savanna country, climbing trees in jungles, swimming in the open seas, diving into the freshwaters of continental rivers, or digging holes deep into the earth. Any-

Salvator monitor

where their prey goes, these lizards seem capable of following. They eat almost anything they can find and catch. Their diet seems limited only by their relative size. Small or young monitors eat insects, worms, fish, eggs, and little creatures such as mice and birds. As they grow larger they will attack and eat monkeys, large birds, small pigs, and even deer. Most monitors are known to be cannibalistic, eating their own young, and all of them are partial to eggs and carrion.

The Komodo dragon (*Varanus komodoensis*) grows to be the largest and heaviest lizard in the world. It has been known to reach almost ten feet in length and weigh close to 300 pounds. Despite this large size, it was not discovered until 1912, probably because it lives only on three small islands—Komodo, Flores, and Ringa of the Lesser Sundas, which are located between Australia and Borneo.

Once discovered, every zoo in the world desired one for its collection. Oddly enough, although extremely fierce and dangerous on their native islands, the "dragon" becomes quite docile in captivity, and demand soon exceeded supply. To prevent extinction, protective laws had to go into effect.

The destructive ability of this giant monitor was well demonstrated some years ago when Sam Dunton, then the staff photographer for the New York Zoological Society, went into the cage to photograph a pair of them. One of the lizards reached up and placed a clawed foot

Monitor claws

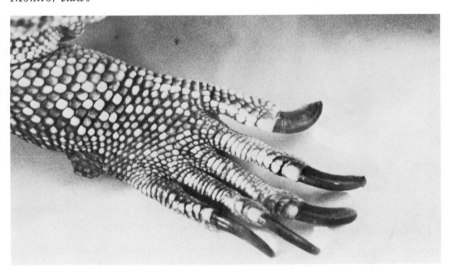

on Sam's leg, much as a friendly puppy would do. Then it used this foot as a prop to raise its forebody. Its weight was such that the claws slid down, ripping both pants and leg, destroying the pants and re-

24

quiring about sixty stitches to mend the leg. This was entirely unintentional. At a later date, I visited these same monitors and felt rather concerned as both of them walked casually over to meet me. They stopped right next to me and allowed me to pet their heads, both of which were knee-high. Each then ran out a foot of black tongue to check my odor, and each allowed me to slap it affectionately upon the shoulders.

Newly hatched Komodo monitors spend much of their early life in trees, catching insects for food and avoiding the ground-dwelling, cannibalistic adults. When large and strong enough to compete, they descend to the ground, and become voracious hunters of game. If the prey is too large to be swallowed whole, the "dragon" either shakes it apart or tears it into smaller chunks with its teeth and claws. By

Young Salvator monitor in tree

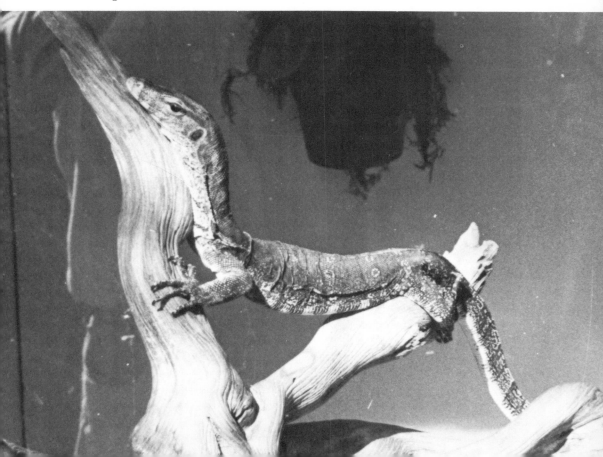

shaking, tearing, and ripping, large monitors can reduce and swallow an entire half-grown deer, head, hide, bones, and all. It then retires to a safe spot and spends the next few days resting, while its strong stomach juices digest the meal completely.

The second largest monitor, *Varanus salvator*, lives throughout a vast area. It is called the water monitor, or kabaragoya, and its domain stretches from India to the islands of the Pacific. It seems about equally at home on land or in either freshwater or saltwater and has added fish to the normal varied lizard diet. It has been seen by sailors many miles out at sea. Swimming with its legs held parallel to its sides, and its strong tail waving back and forth, the lizard sculls with apparent ease.

The seven- to eight-foot Nile monitor (*Varanus niloticus*) is from Africa. It, too, is a water monitor, but lives near the freshwaters of that continent. This lizard digs burrows in the riverbanks for its home, and makes underwater entrances. It is quite fond of crocodile eggs which are buried in large clusters under riverbank soil and sand. The monitor sniffs them out with its long tongue and Jacobson's organs. It then starts to dig them out for a meal, unless interrupted by a guardian female crocodile which, if possible, makes a meal out of the monitor.

Australia is home to several species of monitors. Although a bit smaller, they are equally ferocious, agile, and carnivorous. Most species dig snug holes in the soil where they hide from excessive heat or which they use as a haven in times of danger. Their smaller size and less weight enable them to climb trees better than the giants, and they spend much time up there searching for birds, eggs, lizards, or small mammals.

Of the smaller-bodied, longer-tailed, tree-climbing varieties of monitors, none is more beautiful than the dexterous green monitor (*Varanus prasinus*) of New Guinea. This all-green lizard may grow

26

Above: *Close-up of the head of a green tree monitor*   Below: *Green tree monitor*

to almost a yard in length and has a prehensile tail, one that, like a monkey's tail, can coil about a limb and aid the monitor in hanging on.

Monitors reproduce by laying eggs. Most deposit them in clusters under the soil, but a few tree varanids place their eggs in rotted tree trunks or stumps. The most unique area is utilized by the Nile monitor. The female has been known to tear a hole in a large termite nest where she then lays her eggs. The termites soon seal up the opening to maintain the proper temperature and humidity for them, which is also adequate for hatching monitor eggs. When the eggs hatch, the well-clawed young immediately tear their way out.

All the monitors have excellent eyesight, acute hearing, and a keen sense of smell—all of which aid them in their quests for food. Many of them seem to prefer raiding local farms and, with their climbing and digging abilities, no fence can keep them out. Their chief prey are the chickens and eggs which can easily and quickly be picked up and swallowed. Some larger lizards also take young pigs and sheep. When possible, farmers greet them with a shotgun, but a fast-running, dodging monitor makes a poor target.

Other than occasional cannibalism, the chief enemy of the monitors is man. Natives of some areas use these lizards for food and many tribes use monitor skins for their drumheads.

3

THE CHAMELEONS

Family Chamaeleonidae

Of the eighty species of chameleons, the great majority are found in Africa and Madagascar. One or two species also inhabit southern Asia, India, and a few of the islands in the Mediterranean. There are no true chameleons in the New World. The little American "chameleon" is actually an iguanid (*Anolis carolinensis*).

Whether judged by appearance or actions, the chameleon is probably the oddest or most unique of all lizards. Most are so highly specialized for life in the trees that they rarely leave them and can barely walk, or even eat, while on the ground. Their food is basically insects, but occasionally they will eat small lizards.

Chameleon feet seem to have divided palms or soles, but in reality it is their toes that oppose each other. Three long toes on one side directly oppose two on the other. Toes like this can be wrapped around a branch tightly enough to withstand the strongest winds. Furthermore, most chameleons have long, prehensile tails that can coil tightly about a limb to act as a fifth hand.

Their eyes are equally specialized. The eyes are mounted in the tips of fleshy, turretlike, mobile mounds. Each eye moves independently of the other, so one turret can be aiming directly ahead while the other can be pivoted around to peer behind. If one eye focuses on an insect, the other swings around immediately to focus on the same target. The

European chameleon with coiled tail, grasping toes, and turret eyes

Eye of European chameleon

widely separated eyes enable the lizard to determine the exact distance from the insect to the end of its nose.

Because chameleons are undoubtedly the slowest and most deliberate moving of all lizards, they need something special to catch such fast prey as insects. They have it. Their tongue is like no other tongue in the Animal Kingdom. When extended, it is almost as long or, in some species, longer than the reptile's body. When not in use, it is pulled back into the mouth and pleated over a cartilage rod much as one can push a silk stocking over an extended arm. Muscles hold it there.

When distance and aim are determined, the chameleon exerts considerable muscular pressure on the base of the folded tongue, and at the same time releases the holding muscles. Just as a wet watermelon

31

seed can be shot out with pressure between two fingers, so is the re-leased tongue ejected. At its tip there is an enlarged portion that se-cretes a sticky substance that traps the insect upon contact. All the lizard must do now is reel in the tongue, stack it neatly upon the car-tilage rod, swallow the insect, and reset the holding muscles. The tongue becomes so limp, once it has captured an insect, that it dangles down as the reptile pulls it back. If the lizard eats while on the ground, the tongue is dragged back with all sorts of dirt and debris stuck to it.

The word "chameleon" means changeable, and these reptiles can change the colors of their skin quite rapidly. The color changes are made because of emotion or physical discomfort more than, as popu-larly believed, to create a camouflage against different backgrounds. On cool days, the lizard will affect a dark-colored skin because a darker color absorbs more warmth from the sun's rays. Light colors reflect the sun, so the skin will be lighter-colored on bright, warm days. Very dark, drab colors often denote that the lizard is not well.

Such color changes are made possible by millions of tiny pigment cells that are embedded in the skin. By expanding some and contract-ing other cells, the skin can become almost white, brown, green, yel-low, or even black. Some days, when the sun filters through leaves and branches cast their shadows, the chameleon's skin becomes many-colored, or mottled, to counteract the varying degrees of temperature on its body.

Occasionally chameleons are seen traveling across the ground. It becomes necessary now and then for one or more to leave a certain grove of trees and shrubs to find a more suitable clump. Food may be scarce because of too many lizards, or they may be looking for mates. On the ground they move faster than they do in the trees, undoubtedly

Top: *European chameleon shedding*
Center and bottom: *Color phases of European chameleon*

because they are out of their element and more vulnerable to enemies. Their gait is rambling and awkward because of their unusual feet. Chameleons also descend to the ground to lay their eggs. A dozen or more may be buried in holes scooped out of the soil.

East Africa is home to one of the more spectacular species, Jackson's chameleon (*Chamaeleo jacksonii*). Although only five to seven inches long from nose to tip of tail, it manages to look formidable. Three stout horns project from the front of the male's head and curve outward and up. The horns almost look vicious. A female has much smaller, almost inconspicuous horns. These horns are normally used only in disputes over territory or battling for a mate, and even then produce no injuries but merely push an antagonist backward or occasionally off its perch. Some natives have been known to cut off and grind up the horns to be used in home medicines.

Most chameleons are egg layers but Jackson's chameleons give birth to anywhere from thirty to forty living young at a time.

The eight- to ten-inch common chameleon of North Africa (*Chamaeleo chamaeleon*) has several subspecies that inhabit southern Europe, southwestern Asia, and India. Among them they almost encircle the Mediterranean Sea. As their name implies, they are common, not only in the wild but also in the zoos of the world. Due to the North African terrain, which is desert or semidesert with sparse vegetation, the African chameleon spends more time on the ground than in the few trees or shrubs. It has even taken to digging and living in holes, and dines mainly on ground insects such as locusts and grasshoppers.

Like most chameleons, this one is extremely territorial and disputes any opposition by another lizard of the same species. In cages, where more than one male is present, there are usually several confrontations each day. The aggressor announces his intentions by puffing his body full of air, standing sideways, and rocking back and forth. If the transgressor is of near or equal size, a fight composed of biting and shov-

34

Jackson's chameleon

ing may occur. If there is too much difference in size, the smaller one normally exhales all possible air and retreats.

Another common chameleon, the flap-necked (*Chamaeleo dilepis*), is found in South Africa. It is slightly larger than the previous species, growing occasionally to over a foot in length, and is equally common in captivity. Its name, flap-necked chameleon, was given it because of

Flap-necked chameleon

two fleshy protuberances projecting from the head, just behind the eyes. These fleshy appendages can be erected and seem to be used to denote excitement or anger.

The island of Madagascar has, among its many species of chameleons, both the largest and the smallest of these lizards. Oustalet's chameleon (*Chamaeleo oustaleti*) reaches about two feet in length and is capable of seizing mice and young birds with its tongue. The smallest chameleons, and probably one of the smallest of all lizards, are the inch-and-a-half-long *Brookesia minima* from a small island

36

off the coast of Madagascar and *Brookesia tuberculata* from the Madagascar mainland. All the lizards of the genus *Brookesia* are small and their tails are too short to be prehensile, meaning that they cannot coil the tail around a branch to provide additional support as most chameleons do. They spend much of their time on the ground hunting for insects amid the leaves and other forest litter.

In South Africa, a four-inch-long chameleon, *Microsaura pumila* or Pygmy chameleon, gained a bit of notoriety when a German scientist discovered that it has the ability to store sperm. This is not unique in reptiles, as the North American prairie rattlesnake is known to have the same ability, but the Pygmy chameleon seems to be the first lizard known to be so endowed. This ability allows the lizard to mate when the opportunity arises but give birth at a later time, when climatic conditions should be at their best.

The uniqueness of the Pygmy chameleon does not stop here, however. When giving birth to her live young, the female does not deposit them upon the ground as most live-bearing lizards do. Instead, she glues each embryonic sac containing a young chameleon to a branch of the tree or shrub to which she clings. Only one act mars her reputation. Once in a while as she snaps out her tongue for food, she secures and consumes one of her own offspring.

4
THE IGUANAS

Family Iguanidae

The iguanas make up a large family comprising almost 700 species of lizards. With the exception of three little-known species, all of them are found in the New World, that is, North, Central, and South America. Iguanas range from four inches to six feet in length and inhabit about every type of environment, from the southern tip of South America well up into Canada, and many coastal islands.

Oddly enough, there is another large family of lizards, the Agamidae, that parallels the Iguanidae in both appearance and habits but lives in most of the other half of the world. Many of them so closely resemble the iguanas that they can be told apart only by geographic distribution and their teeth arrangement. Agamid teeth are attached to the top of the jawbone just as our own are and are called acrodont. Iguanid teeth are attached to the inner surface of the jawbone and are called pleurodont.

Many iguanas can also be identified by a curious habit. During courtship or when confronting another male over territory, they will rear up on their front legs and bob up and down, much like a human doing push-ups.

One of the largest and most regal-looking iguanas lives in the jungle areas of Mexico and South America. A few escapees from local owners

Common iguana

have also colonized southern Florida in recent years. The common iguana (*Iguana iguana*) grows to be about six feet long, over half of which is a long tapering tail that is capable of dispensing a severe blow. Being a fruit and foliage eater, it is frequently found high in trees, satisfying its appetite or merely stretched out on a limb sunning itself. It is this second habit that makes common iguanas excellent exhibits in zoos. They will pose for hours, looking alert, but not moving. Small highway sideshows used to mislabel them Chinese dragons.

Unfortunately for the larger iguanas, their flesh is tasty to man; in fact, the native populations of iguana country use them as a basic food. They have been so depleted that these lizards are now protected.

Despite its size, the common iguana is a fast lizard. On the ground it can outrun most dogs. Like a squirrel, it can scamper up trees or, in populated areas, even climb telephone poles. It can jump from considerable heights and hit the ground uninjured, or run or dive into water where it is an excellent swimmer. If caught, it becomes a mean antagonist. Strong jaws, crushing and tearing teeth, and long claws are encountered only after one gets past the slashing tail. The common iguana has a fringe of leathery scales running from just behind the head, down the top of its back to just beyond the base of the tail. From here to the end of the tail, these scales grow smaller but harder and sharper. A good blow not only can knock an enemy off balance, but may inflict a painful wound.

Some years before protective laws prohibited their collection and sale, the Black Hills Reptile Gardens imported a number of these iguanas each year from field collectors and allowed them to roam free in the dome-covered jungle area of the Gardens. People walked through paths that circled the jungle palms, flowering plants, and large trees that gave the exhibit authenticity. Although the lizards quickly tamed down, climbed the trees and posed as naturally and harmlessly as possible, their arrival was something else. Each lizard, when released from its shipping crate, had to be deticked. All had many large blood-sucking ticks attached to every area the lizard could not scratch. To detick a practically fresh-caught, wild, six-foot lizard was exciting. They fought us during the entire operation. We wore long-sleeved leather jackets to ward off their claws. We held them by the heads to avoid being bitten, and we tried to avoid the lashing tail. Once, when working without a jacket, one lizard hit me across the back with a vicious swing of its tail, cutting through my shirt and requiring medicine for the long, smarting cut in my back.

There are several other species of large iguanas in the world, two of which live on the Galápagos Islands, which are located about 600 miles off the coast of Ecuador on the equator. These islands are renowned for their wildlife, little of which is found anywhere else in the world. The largest of the iguanas found here is called the land iguana (*Conolophus subcristatus*) and closely resembles the common iguana. It reaches about four feet in length. Due to a hot, dry climate and soil composed mainly of hard, volcanic rock, there is little foliage other than cactus, which these iguanas eat, spines and all.

The marine iguana (*Amblyrhynchus cristatus*) has a unique feeding habit. It is slightly smaller than the land iguana and has a blunt nose. This sea iguana lives in great colonies on the rocky beaches of some of the Galápagos Islands. Its entire diet consists of seaweed and algae that grow on the rocks from the tidal zone to depths of fifty feet. Each morning, after being warmed by the sun, the lizards slip beneath the waves and swim to their algae and seaweed beds where they crop the weeds off the rocks. Sea iguanas can stay underwater for at least ten minutes before rising to the surface for air. Many zoos have tried in vain to keep marine iguanas on exhibit.

Due to the dryness of the islands where they are found, neither of these lizards can readily obtain sufficient fresh drinking water. The land iguana gains most of its liquids from the cactus it eats. The ma-

41

Rhinoceros iguana

rine iguana drinks seawater, but has glands that distill the excess salt from the bloodstream and blow it out the nose as necessary.

The island of Hispanola, in the Caribbean Sea, is home to another large species of iguana. Because of one or two short, heavy horns located on its nose, it is appropriately named the rhinoceros iguana (*Cyclura cornuta*). A large bulge on the back of the head, a robust body, and the horns give it a rather sinister appearance. It is almost as tough as it looks. It does not grow to be as long as the common species, but is heavier and far more aggressive. The Haitians hunt it for food and use dogs to track down or occasionally catch it, but the

42

Spiny-tailed iguana

iguana is usually more than a match for the dog. It is not a tree-climber but spends most of its time on the ground eating vegetation or whatever bird and animal life it can catch. It lives in holes that it digs in the tough, coral, rocky soil of the island.

One species of another genus of large iguanas occasionally reaches into the United States. The spiny-tailed iguana (*Ctenosaura pectinata*) can sometimes be found in the south Texas area around Big Bend. This and several other species of three-to-four-foot-long *Ctenosaura* lizards range through Mexico and Central America. Some of these were once released in the jungle area of the Reptile Gardens, along

43

Anolis

with the green iguana, but were quickly recaptured and removed. Instead of resting peacefully on tree limbs, they hunted and caught our free-flying birds, raided nestlings, and even challenged visitors.

It is not known how, or when, but three little-known specimens of iguanas traveled far from the normal range. Two types inhabit the island of Madagascar off the coast of East Africa, one of the genus *Chalarodon* and the other of the genus *Oplurus*. A third specimen, *Brachylophus fasciatus*, is found on the little Fiji and Tonga islands of the South Pacific Ocean. Some scientists believe that many years ago the iguanas inhabited much of the Old World and that these three lizard species are only remnants, that they did not travel, but merely hung on. It is strange to find iguanids in agamid territory, and yet there are no agamids on Madagascar and only one species on Fiji.

Not too many years ago, every circus or carnival in America had salesmen who peddled little five-inch, green or brown lizards that were commonly called chameleons. For twenty-five cents, one could purchase one of these little "pets" and tether it to one's shirt by a small chain attached to its collar. These miscalled chameleons are in reality iguanas, *Anolis carolinensis*, and are found throughout most of the southeastern United States.

Unfortunately for the "chameleons," of the thousands upon thousands that were sold, very few survived for long. Most purchasers were told to provide their pets with a little dish of sugar water and feed them dead flies or ant eggs bought in pet shops. But they will rarely touch either. They normally obtain their moisture by lapping drops of rain or dew from the leaves of plants, and are interested in no food that is not alive and moving.

Its misnomer "chameleon" was derived from the lizard's ability to change quickly from brown to green. A cold or ill *Anolis carolinensis* is brown. When feeling good, the color is vivid green. Seldom does it exceed seven inches in length. It spends most of its time in trees and

45

Anolis clinging to vertical pane of glass, showing suction pads.

shrubs where, with a fast rush and open mouth, it stalks and catches insects. Its toes are equipped with both claws and small suction pads that allow it to walk on shiny smooth leaves or windowpanes, or to cling to rough surfaces such as tree bark.

Like most iguanas, all the anolis bob their challenge to any male that disputes their territory. They also wear a loose flap of skin under the throat and, like the larger iguanas, erect this flap or dewlap either in challenge or to aid in attracting a mate. When the dewlap is erected by the "chameleon," it turns pink.

46

Most species of anolis descend to the ground to lay their eggs, either singly or in small groups. *Anolis carolinensis* lays a pair of football-shaped eggs that are only a quarter of an inch long. They hatch into miniature replicas of the adult.

Anolis eggs

The genus *Anolis* is a large one with about 300 species living in the tropical areas between Florida and southern South America. At least two species from the Caribbean Islands have been introduced into Florida and have done well. One, the crested anolis (*Anolis crista-tellus*) is only eight inches long, and wears a low crest along its upper tail surface. The second is the knight anolis (*Anolis equestris*). This large, twenty-inch-long lizard comes from Cuba and has a low, erec-tile crest running down its back.

The western side of the South American continent is basically moun-

47

Above: *Cuban or knight anolis* Below: *Close-up of the head of a Texas horned lizard*

tains and cool climates, not really tropical, and not normally associated with the average lizard. Yet, one genus of many species has made its home in this area. The genus *Liolaemus* is quite large, and all its members live in these high areas. *Liolaemus multiformis* lives close to 16,000 foot elevation, and *Liolaemus magellanicus* lives at the southern tip of South America. Of all lizards, this one resides closest to the Antarctic Circle.

The deserts of the American Southwest are a veritable paradise for lizard lovers. There are many types of small, harmless iguanids to be seen, or even caught if one is both agile and lucky. The genus *Phrynosoma*, or the horned lizards, are perhaps the most frequently captured of the desert lizards. They are often called horned toads, but they are definitely lizards and are not restricted to the Southwest. One species, the short-horned lizard, can be found all the way from Mexico into Canada.

The bodies of all the genus *Phrynosoma* are short, wide, and flat, with short legs and tails. Crowning their heads are varying numbers and lengths of horns fashioned from elongated scales. Covering the back, tail, and legs are usually more, but shorter, hornlike scales, and a fringe of prickly scales often edges the area where the back and undersides meet. There are several different species, each known by the type, length, and number of horns and spiky fringes.

Horned lizards obtain their moisture by eating insects, usually ants, or by lapping up dew or raindrops whenever possible. They do most of their hunting in the mornings and evenings when it's cooler, although horned lizards like more heat than many other desert species. When it becomes too hot for even these heat lovers, the lizards hide under shady shrubs and cactus pads, or bury under the sand. Some species of horned lizards lay eggs, burying them in the soil, while others give birth to living young. It's usually the lizards of the southern range that lay eggs; the long warm season gives them time to incubate and

49

hatch. In the northern range, where summer is shorter, the lizards give birth to living young.

The short-horned lizard (*Phrynosoma douglassi*), along with several subspecies, inhabits much of western United States from Canada south into Mexico. I have caught and kept many of these four- to five-inch lizards in western South Dakota, keeping them alive with ants, mealworms, and flies that had been shaken in a bottle until too stunned to fly. In time, my pets presented me with several broods of young that were about the size of a dime.

The three largest and thorniest "horned toads" reach a length of between six and seven inches. The largest is the Texas horned lizard (*Phrynosoma cornutum*) of Texas and the adjacent states. Slightly smaller is the California or Coast horned lizard (*Phrynosoma coronatum*) that occupies most of western California. Finally, there is the regal horned lizard (*Phrynosoma solare*) of Arizona. All three extend their range south into Mexico, and all three wear head spines that are long and plentiful.

Despite their elongated scales or horns, these little lizards have enemies and are occasionally captured and eaten by birds such as the roadrunner. Some snakes and mammals also try to feast on horned lizards. With their flat bodies and short legs, horned lizards look slow, but when necessary they can move surprisingly fast. If caught, they use a trick or two that often wins them their freedom. One is to inflate themselves with air to look much larger than they really are. The tightened or stretched skin tends to erect more horny scales, making them look too large and prickly to be swallowed. If this accomplishes nothing, they can rupture a blood vessel in the eye and spurt out a few drops of blood in another effort to surprise and make the enemy let go.

Top: *Short-horned lizard* Center: *Newborn short-horned lizard on a dime* Bottom: *Coachwhip snake looking over a horned lizard*

Horned lizards have always been about as popular a pet as the little American chameleon and fare about as poorly in captivity. Their ideal temperature is unduly hot for humans and the average home temperature will be too cold for them to function properly. The preferred food is ants—live active ants, and in quantity. Most homeowners would refuse to release a bottle of live ants in the home, however tight the exhibit cage.

The wild horned lizard is hard to see unless it moves. Each species has colors that closely match those of its surroundings, and when it flattens out on the ground it becomes almost invisible. When frightened, it runs for the nearest patch of cactus or rock pile where it hides or squirms to where a captor cannot reach it. If cornered, however, it can be readily and safely picked up. It is perfectly harmless.

Another genus of iguanids (*Crotaphytus*) roams the plains of Texas, New Mexico, and the adjacent states and they are not so easily

Texas horned lizard

Collared lizard

caught. The collared lizard (*Crotaphytus collaris*) is only a foot long but in some ways it acts like a little dinosaur. It does not depend upon camouflaging coloration to protect itself but rather high speed, extreme versatility dodging, and a substantial bite if cornered. It is readily recognized by the twin black collars that almost completely encircle the neck. Its coloration is variable, being well spotted with reds, yellows, or browns usually against a blue or red-brown background.

Watching one run at high speed, whether in pursuit of food or avoiding an enemy, is interesting. It starts moving on all fours, but after it gains speed, it stands on its hind legs, elevates its tail as a counterbalance, and dodges and weaves, sending up little spurts of sand as each foot falls.

Another dinosaur equivalent is the appetite of the collared lizard. It will eat insects, little snakes and lizards, birds, mice, or about anything else it can catch and dominate. At times, its food seems too large to be swallowed, but the lizard overcomes this obstacle by pushing the food down with its front feet.

The leopard lizard (*Gambelia wislizenii*) is very similar in habits to the collared lizard. Its range includes Texas, but it goes farther west to California and north to Oregon. It lacks the twin collars, is basically tan, and has varying-sized leopardlike dark spots covering much of its body. Although I have never seen it happen, it is said that the leopard lizard will run across an area at full speed chasing a low-flying insect and, at the right time, jump into the air and grasp it in its jaws. Both these lizards and their subspecies are good captives, but must be kept alone. Any smaller cage mates will disappear.

One of the least likely places for a lizard to live is on the slopes of the barren, windblown sand dunes of southern California and western Arizona. This is, however, where three species of eight-inch-long iguanas are found, and nowhere else. Here the temperatures vary from zero degrees F. in winter, to above 150 degrees F. in summer. The winds frequently whip up clouds of fine, choking sand and slowly move the dunes from one area to another. The little iguanas travel with them.

The uma lizard (*Uma notata*) seems well adapted to this environ-

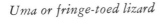

Uma or fringe-toed lizard

ment. It has a fringe of flat scales on the toes of its hind feet that enables it to travel over the loose sand, much as snowshoes aid man in deep, loose snow. Indeed, even better. The lizard has been clocked running over the dunes at better than twenty miles an hour.

During the frequent sandstorms, uma can comfortably see through its protective transparent nictitating membranes, and can close skin flaps over its ear openings and its nostrils. Its lower jaw fits neatly into the top jaw to help keep the sand out.

When in danger, uma runs and dodges, then quickly dives under the

Uma, showing fringes on rear toes

sand where, by wriggling its body and tail, it "swims" through the sand to a, hopefully, safe place.

Technically known as uma, this lizard and its two subspecies are variously called sand swimmer, sand diver, ocellated lizard, fringed-toed, or just simply sand lizard. It survives by eating any insects that may venture up on the dunes, or an occasional leaf from the sparse vegetation found at the edges of the dunes.

Where California, Nevada, Utah, and Arizona meet, and extending into Mexico, there are dry but rocky deserts that are the home territory of the peaceful, flower-eating chuckwalla (*Sauromalus obesus*). It is a drab-colored, chunky, lazy, rock-climber. This sixteen-inch-long lizard spends much of its time sunning atop its favorite rock pile. If the weather should become too hot, it retreats into the shady cool openings beneath the pile. Its shape, wide but flat, and its exceptionally short legs, make it possible to squeeze into crevices seemingly too narrow to accept it. Even when lying on an open rock, it is hard to see, due to its protective colors of red, brown, and gray almost perfectly matching its favorite rock pile.

Chuckwallas are as peaceful as they look and rarely, if ever, bite. If frightened, the lizard will crawl down the rocks and wriggle its body as deeply as possible into some narrow crack where it is almost impossible to pull it out. It then inflates its body with air, jamming the scales against the rocks to hold onto every irregularity. Oddly enough, it often allows its tail to hang outside the crack.

There is an old desert story that claims that a traveler, if out of water and food, can refresh himself by catching and eating a chuckwalla. There will be ample food and moisture within such a lizard. The trick is to get one out of its crack, but once the technique is learned, there is no problem. Fasten a cactus needle to a stick. Hold the lizard by the tail, puncture the body with the needle to deflate it, and pull it out.

56

Chuckwalla

Chuckwallas are completely herbacious, eating only flowers, leaves, and buds. I have kept them on a diet of dandelions, plus both alfalfa leaves and flowers.

Another placid iguana inhabits much the same area as the chuck-walla but this one spends most of its time on the shrubs and trees or browsing between the rocky outcroppings. Although a plant eater, it

57

Desert iguana

does add a few insects and spiders to its diet. It is called the desert iguana (*Dipsosaurus dorsalis*) and is about the same length as the chuckwalla, but much more slender and lighter in weight. Its basic colors are a mottled gray and tan. It has a series of black bars ringing its tail and wears a low crest of keeled scales down its back and along the top of its tail.

This lizard loves heat, and long after most desert creatures have hidden under the sand or desert debris, the desert iguana is still out searching for food. It has been seen when temperatures hovered about

58

Zebra-tailed lizard being eaten by a patch-nosed snake

112 degrees F. However, at this temperature, the lizard tends to be high in the bushes to catch any possible breeze.

Unlike the chuckwalla that hides in cracks, a frightened desert iguana dashes to any nearby hole or cactus patch. At night, it retires to a burrow and often plugs the entrance with sand to keep out any predators.

A small but fast lizard of the North American desert is the seven- to nine-inch zebra-tailed or gridiron-tailed lizard (*Callisaurus draco-noides*). This one can be identified by the wide black bands on its tail.

59

Blue spiny lizards

One must look closely to see the two folds of skin that stretch across its throat, and the external ear patches or tympanums. When running it carries the tail curled high over its back.

The gridiron-tailed lizard could easily be confused with the equally active earless lizard (*Cophosaurus texanus*). It too has black bands on its tail and runs with it curled over its back, but this lizard lacks any form of ear opening.

Except for a block of states that extends roughly from the Dakotas east to the Atlantic Ocean and south to New Jersey, the spiny lizards are found in the United States and Mexico.

The spiny lizards belong to the genus *Sceloporus* and are easily recognized, but it takes a professional reptile person, or herpetologist, to separate the thirty-odd species. They are basically small lizards, from three to seven inches long, but a few southern species do attain a foot or so in length. All of them are characteristically colored in grays, browns, and blacks to match the soil, tree bark, or rocks that make up their surroundings. Some species have zigzag streaks of darker colors crossing their backs and most males will wear various-sized patches of blue under their throats, along their sides, or even on their tails. A few also have black collars about their necks.

The name "spiny lizards" is appropriate to them all because they are spiny to both sight and touch. Each scale covering the back, sides, legs, and tail is keeled or has a sharp-edged ridge that runs along the top of the scale and extends beyond as a tiny sharp spine. Their under-body scales are smooth. Another common name is swift lizard, which is also appropriate simply because they are swift. Spiny lizards or swifts are almost impossible to catch. They can run across the ground, along a fence, up a tree trunk, over the thorniest of cactus, or even up and down an apparently smooth wall of rock with incredible speed. Should you grasp one, ten to one all you would have is its tail. Swifts are renowned for dropping their tails in defense.

61

One of the most common of the swifts is the three- to eight-inch eastern spiny or fence lizard (*Sceloporus undulatus*) and its several subspecies. These are found from Arizona to the Atlantic coast and north to South Dakota and east to New Jersey. They are normally called fence lizards since they frequent split rail and pole fences. It is a common sight to see them dashing along the horizontal rails in pursuit of flies and other insects that use the rails as sunny resting places. If alarmed, fence lizards will usually scurry up the trunk of the nearest tree and run around to the opposite side and wait. If you walk around the tree, the lizard does the same, always keeping the tree between you and itself. Where there is something to climb, the fence or spiny lizards will climb it. Another species, *Sceloporus occidentalis*, and its subspecies are equally common in the Pacific states from Oregon to Mexico and west to Nevada and Utah.

Swifts are very territorial but tend to live close to one another. Where you see one, there is a great possibility of many living in that vicinity. Each individual spends its entire life in its own few feet of territory, and on sunny warm days many will be out soaking up the warmth. Such a find is always interesting. Between chasing their insect food, disputing territorial rights with much bobbing and display of color, plus frequent short battles ending with the winner in hot pursuit of the vanquished, there is always considerable activity.

I once spent over an hour trying to get one picture of a little three-inch *Sceloporus* that had an entire cholla cactus in which to hide. This extremely prickly, many-branched, three-foot-tall plant was a perfect playground for the lizard. Just as I lined up the little lizard in the lens, it would jump to another branch, land on the needles, scurry around to the other side, and peer around to watch for my next move. I almost

Top: *Western fence lizard*   Center: *Eastern fence lizard in its western range*
Bottom: *Fence lizards in territorial battle*

wore a path around the plant before I got my one picture, just its head peering around a prickly branch.

Not all swifts are small, nor do they haunt only ledges and forested areas. The blue spiny lizard (*Sceloporus cyanogenys*) reaches almost fifteen inches long and lives in the hot, rocky areas of South Texas

Blue spiny lizard

and Mexico. Another, *Sceloporus graciosus*, is a foot-long desert lover of the Southwest and Mexico. One of the prettiest of them is the ten-inch granite lizard (*Sceloporus orcutti*) of Southern California and Mexico. If seen in the appropriate light, its back seems iridescent with a purplish blue color. It received its common name due to its habit of living close to granite, rocks, and ledges.

The ancient Greeks wrote fanciful tales of both real and imaginary animals. Among these fables is one concerning a monster named the basilisk. This creature, half-lizard and half-some other type of animal, could stare at a person through piercing yellow eyes and turn him into

64

Above: *Granite swift*   Below: *Granite swift with portion of tail missing and beginning to regenerate*

Male and female common basilisk on a wall

stone. In Central America there live three or four species and sub-species of lizards that have piercing eyes and bodies that resemble somewhat this fabled monster, so they are naturally called basilisks.

The modern basilisk is hardly a monster. This harmless lizard grows to be just over thirty inches long, and two-thirds of that length is tail. Its body is slight and its legs are long. Basilisks are easily recognized by the sloping crest on top of the head, another long ridge on the back, and a third along the top of the tail. The males wear very apparent, even outstanding, crests; females have no tail or dorsal crests.

All basilisks have exceptionally long, clawed toes, with the hind toes almost twice the length of the front. Essentially they are tree dwellers, where they are as agile as monkeys, and seek insects and bits of ripe fruit. However, they do descend to the ground to catch and eat small mammals or birds.

Being small and light, they have many enemies in the tropical jungle, so have developed considerable running speed and one renowned trick to elude them. The basilisk is a biped and, when moving fast, runs in an upright position on its hind legs. When pursued by an enemy, it jumps to the ground and heads at full speed for the nearest body of water. Being light of body, long-toed and very fast, it can run right out on and across the surface. Some authorities claim that it can, with a good start, cross up to 100 feet of water without sinking in. When basilisks lose speed, they will sink, but they are excellent swimmers. Some have been known to swim to the bottom and hide.

The common basilisk (*Basiliscus basiliscus*) is a combination of browns and tans with a few dark vertical bars and a white throat and line down its back. Costa Rica is home to the beautiful *Basiliscus plumifrons*, which comes closest to the ancient artist's conception of a basilisk. This all-green lizard has vivid yellow pupils in its piercing eyes, and a double crest on its head.

Some iguanids do not fit the basic idea of how an iguana should act

67

Above: *Common basilisk*   Below: *Plumifrons basilisk*

or even look. In South America there is a tree iguana (*Polychrus acutirostris*) with an elongated body and tail that totals about thirty inches. Its toes and legs are extra long, enabling it to reach for and grasp branches. Its eyes are located in mobile fleshy turrets that rotate, resembling those of the true chameleons. The prehensile tail, which is more than two-thirds of the lizard's length, is more like those of a true chameleon than an iguana.

Another genus, *Corytophanes*, contains several species from Central America. These are four-foot-long tree lizards without prehensile tails. The heads are topped with a crest or helmet that normally lies flat on the lizard's head. If frightened or threatened, the helmet lizard (*Corytophanes cristatus*) raises the crest, puffs out the sides of its neck and extends its dewlap. To an antagonist this could be very frightening.

There are hundreds of other iguanas, but these are the most interesting and representative; the remainder are subspecies and very similar.

5

THE GECKOS

Family Gekkonidae

The geckos are the only "talking" lizards in the world, but they speak only one word, "gecko." At least that is what some of their calls sound like to some people and that is undoubtedly how these lizards received their name. They number somewhere around 500 species and their geographical distribution is the entire tropical and subtropical world. Geckos range in length from only an inch and a half for the ocellated gecko (*Sphaerodactylus argus*) to the foot-long Tokay gecko (*Gekko gecko*). Geckos inhabit all types of territory, from the great rain forests and jungles to the arid, sandy deserts, and some species live permanently in the homes of man.

Geckos have small scales that do not overlap each other, which gives the skin a soft, pliable, almost velvety look and feel. They also have eyes that readily mark them as a gecko. Being mostly night hunters, they need eyes with pupils large enough to see in the dark. However, because such large pupils admit too much light when the sun shines and their enemies are about, the eyes are constructed to serve both needs. In the dark, the pupils are huge round orbs capable of utilizing every bit of available light. During the day the pupils contract into thin vertical slits that shut out most of the light. If necessary the pupils can actually close, with the exception of four pinhole-sized openings.

Most geckos have no eyelids but see through immobile, protective

70

The eye of a Tokay gecko

transparent shields that cover the eyes. These shields are so thin and clear that they are hardly noticeable. They do get dirty now and then and it's interesting to see a gecko run out its long fleshy tongue and, using it as a windshield wiper, clean the surface of each eyeshield.

The toes of most geckos are also different from those of other lizards. They are wide, flat, and extremely flexible. If looked at from the underside, one sees a series of ridges across each toe. Under extreme magnification, each ridge is seen to be equipped with thousands of tiny hooks. By pressing down the toe, the microscopic hooks can secure a

71

hold on most any surface, including a pane of dry window glass. To release the hooks, the toe is merely lifted or bent up from the claw end first, and the entire foot is free. Running up and down house walls or upside down across ceilings is made easy with such toe pads. To travel up rough surfaces, such as the bark of a tree, the geckos also have the conventional claw on each toe.

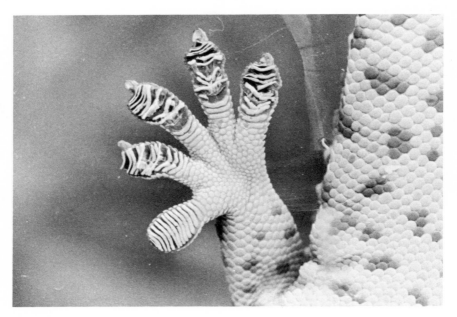

Gecko foot on glass

Hiding away during the daylight hours is the first defense of the gecko. It has such a soft, flat, flexible body that it can easily squeeze into tight crevices or under rocks. House geckos hide behind pictures, shelf objects, or inside cupboards, which makes it interesting for home-owners when they move something.

A second defense is to act tough by standing their ground, open-ing their mouths, hollering "gecko" and, in some cases, actually charg-ing for a foot or two. Although many lizards practice autotomy—the ability to lose a part of the body—geckos seem to be the most consistent. Most lizards do this only if the tail is grasped, but geckos may drop their tails even before being touched. A last and odd defense is used by only a few species of geckos. If grasped, they will actually slough off, or shed, portions of their skin. A collector who reaches down and grasps such a lizard will first be delighted with his catch. As the gecko twists and wriggles free, leaving only patches of skin between the fingers, and the mutilated lizard runs away, the collector is probably horrified. Not only has he lost the lizard, but he has obviously injured it. No permanent harm is done, however. The lizard will, in a few weeks, regrow the lost skin and be as good as new.

Normally, a gecko will lay one or two eggs at a time, although clusters of eggs from some species have been found. Each egg is enclosed in a protective coating and glued to some object. Gecko eggs have been stuck onto the sides of packing cases or other things pending shipment, and have been transported all over the world. Odd

Tokay gecko's eggs in a pebble wall

Tokay gecko on a wall

species of geckos may turn up anywhere. If food and climate are compatible, the young will hatch and mature. If a mate can be found, the species may become permanent. The same thing is true of adult geckos that have hidden in cartons or crates. The original homes of several species of geckos have never been satisfactorily determined.

The largest, most aggressive species is the Tokay gecko (*Gekko gecko*) which is generally distributed throughout the Philippines, Asia, and the Dutch East Indies. Blue-gray in color and speckled in red, this

74

gecko grows to be about one foot long, if the tail is included. It is anything but inoffensive. It has been known to eat mice, little birds, snakes, and lizards, as well as a generous supply of insects. If annoyed or grasped by a human, it immediately attacks with a severe bite and tends to hang on.

One of the men working with me had the fleshy end of a finger bitten off as clean as if sliced with a knife. After being bitten myself, I began using gloves when handling a Tokay, but found that the lizard would not let go. The only way I could make it release the glove was to place both glove and lizard in the cage and later, when the gecko had calmed down, retrieve the glove.

Because tropical homes are often invaded by insects, the gecko too has moved in to take advantage of the good hunting. The homeowners have learned to treasure the gecko, knowing it is catching and eating small unwanted guests. Over the years, people have formed many superstitions concerning this reptile, both good and bad. Some owners of a new home wait impatiently for the first gecko to move in, believing that the sooner it arrives, the luckier the home will be. Harmful superstitions are that the gecko is poisonous or that it spreads leprosy.

There are several other ceiling runners such as the common house gecko (*Hemidactylus frenatus*) and the sad gecko (*Lepidodactylus lugubris*), but all are smaller and more gentle than the Tokay.

One of the better tricksters among geckos is named Kuhl's fringed gecko (*Ptychozoon kuhlii*). It is also called the flying gecko or parachute gecko, due to its actions. It is not easily seen. Kuhl's gecko lives on the island of Java in the Dutch East Indies. Native Javanese claim they have seen this lizard fly, or at least parachute to the ground.

Looking closely at one that is flattened against a tree limb, it can be seen that skin flaps on either side of the head are open and pressed down against the bark. More "wings" or flaps extend out from either side of the lizard's midsection, and even the legs have narrow flaps

75

Above: *Flying geckos*—Ptychozoon kuhli *(upper) and* Ptychozoon lionatom *(lower)*
Below: Ptychozoon lionatom

reaching down the full length of each side. The tail is scalloped on both sides with smaller flaps, and even the toes wear flaps that give the foot the appearance of being webbed. With flaps extended and pressed against the tree, the broken outline and color forms an almost perfect camouflage.

Although it could probably glide or parachute to the ground, this reptile could never fly. There are no bones to support the flaps and no muscles to cause them to move up and down. There are three species of "flying" geckos in the Dutch East Indies and one in the Philippines.

Occasionally, when one turns over rocks or desert debris of our southwestern desert areas, he will discover a delicate-looking four- to six-inch lizard that wears dark bands over the back and tail. This will undoubtedly be one of the three species of our native geckos. It has the huge eyes and velvety skin of all geckos, but differs in having eyelids. Even when open, the lids are apparent, due to a protruding ridge that surrounds each eye. It differs also in that it has no pads or disks on its narrow toes, only tiny claws.

These banded geckos, as they are commonly called, are harmless, gentle little prowlers that eat whatever insects and spiders the desert provides. The Texas banded gecko (*Coleonyx brevis*) can be found in southern Texas and down into Mexico. The Big Bend banded gecko (*Coleonyx variegatus*) is found in Arizona, Southern California, and down into Mexico.

If a person intends to capture a banded gecko he should be careful. The gecko will more than likely drop its tail regardless of where you grasp it. They do well in captivity, but normally remain hidden all day, coming out to eat only after dark.

For those Americans who truly like to watch geckos in the wild, visit Florida. There are approximately seven species found there, all of which have been introduced. The most common, the Mediterranean

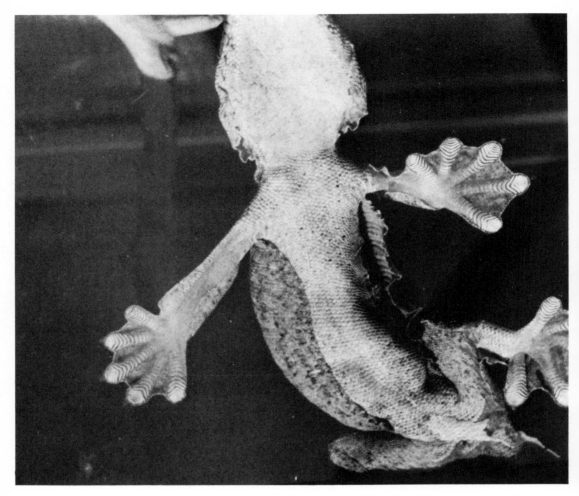

Flying gecko on a pane of glass showing webbed feet and closed skin flaps

gecko (*Hemidactylus turcicus*), has the greatest range, being found throughout most of southern and central Florida. It is also called the Turkish gecko, from its point of origin in the countries around the Mediterranean Sea, and has also been transported into southern Texas, Louisiana, and into South America. The Turkish gecko is one of the house-dwelling, ceiling runners that people have grown used to and

78

accept kindly where it is native. It grows no longer than five inches, and perhaps someday Americans will also realize that geckos are excellent insect catchers in the home.

Smaller but prettier is the yellow-head gecko (*Gonatodes albogularis*) that seldom exceeds three inches. It can easily be recognized by its yellow head, white-tipped tail, and sharp-pointed toes. Introduced from South America, it can now be found around the southern tip of Florida.

In the same area are the ashy gecko (*Sphaerodactylus cinereus*), the tiny one-and-a-half-inch reef gecko (*Sphaerodactylus notatus*), and the ocellated species named for its white speckles (*Sphaerodactylus argus*). All are from the Caribbean Islands.

The Namib Desert of southwestern Africa is an area of loose sand on which it is difficult to travel, yet a gecko lives there. The webbed-footed gecko (*Palmatogecko rangei*) leads a life similar to the sand dune lizards of the United States. Instead of fringed toes, its webbed feet enable it to dash over the loose sand or dive under it and, by "swimming," escape potential enemies. Another oddity concerning this lizard is the skin. It is so thin and pale white in color that one can practically look through it and into its body and see its internal organs.

With so many species of geckos, it is not surprising that there are many variations. Some dig and spend much of their time in holes in the ground. One digging species, *Ptenopus garrulus* of South Africa, makes such a racket, chirping and clucking at each other, that it has been given the name of the garrulous or talking lizard. The concert usually starts at sundown, just before the geckos go out hunting.

On the island of Madagascar there are numerous species of geckos that inhabit the trees. Most are green in color and one, *Phelsuma madagascariensis*, is vivid green with bright red markings. Unlike most geckos, these add fruit and the sweetness of flower nectar to their diet. Furthermore, they are diurnal, hunting in the daylight.

There seems to be no habitat in the warmer parts of the world where geckos cannot be found. Geckos have been seen on board ships, airplanes, rock walls, in homes, deserts, trees, tropical forests, and one species, *Alsophylax tibetanus*, is found high in the Himalayan Mountains.

6

THE AGAMIDS

Family Agamidae

The agamids are frequently called the Old World counterparts of the New World iguana lizards, and with many species this is indeed true. Some agamids look so much like iguanids that they can be distinguished only because they live in the Old World, where, with the exception of three species, no iguanas are found. Furthermore, all agamids have acrodont teeth; the teeth are attached to the top of the jaw bone.

There are about 300 species and subspecies in the family. They can be found throughout an enormous area, practically the entire Old World. Agamids vary from about five inches to three feet long and frequent a great diversity of habitats; some are semiaquatic, others live in trees or on the ground, and a few even choose the hottest and driest of deserts.

The most unlikely place to find a lizard is in the air, yet there are several species of the genus *Draco* that are quite capable of sustained flights or, rather, glides. The "flying dragon" of Indonesia is not at all spectacular when at rest and is only eight or so inches in length, spindly of body, and colored to match the branch on which it lies. However, when in pursuit of insects for food, or avoiding an enemy, the "dragon" immediately lives up to its name. Several elongated ribs suddenly fan out from its body, spreading out highly colored, thin skin coverings that act as adequate wings. A strong jump into the air propels the lizard much like launching a paper airplane and results in substantially long gliding flights to another perch. The rib muscles that control the wings allow only for lateral movement; thus there can be no flapping, or actual flying. Observers say that the draco can move so fast that when securing a nearby flying insect, the opening of the wings, the jump, the catch, return to the branch, and folding of the wings takes but a single moment.

The most common species of flying dragon, *Draco volans,* lives in Malaya and the Philippines. There are about fifteen other species found throughout the islands of Indonesia, and one species, *Draco dussumieri,* in southern India.

In New Guinea and northern Australia there is a thirty-inch lizard that might well be called a bluffer rather than by its ponderous scientific name of *Chlamydosaurus kingii.* Like the draco, this lizard when relaxed is not too exciting. Although almost three feet long, twenty inches of that is a long tapering tail. When threatened, it assumes a far different appearance and even an experienced herpetologist will have second thoughts about grasping it.

This lizard's first reaction to danger is to run. It begins running on four legs but when sufficient speed has been attained, it will rear up on its hind legs and, with its tail straight out behind to aid in balancing, it will run a weaving course for some distance. When it feels safe, it will stop and look back; if the enemy is still in sight, it runs again. This may happen several times, but when it begins to tire, and the danger remains, it will enter plan two of its defensive procedures.

Suddenly it stops and faces the enemy. Its mouth will gape wide open, exposing a red interior, and a fan of colorful skin will be erected about its neck. The tail will thrash from side to side in a threatening gesture, and instead of a thirty-inch, frightened, average-looking lizard, the enemy now faces a dangerous-looking, apparently ferocious, large antagonist.

82

Camouflaged draco on a tree branch

Due to this frill or fan about its neck, the lizard is commonly called the frilled lizard. The erected frill on a full-grown male may be as much as, and occasionally more than, nine inches in diameter. Long bones attached to the neck region move and support the frill. When it is relaxed, they lay parallel to the neck. The frill is neatly plaited, out of the way, and to the unsuspecting, practically invisible. Frilled lizards are all bluff, but good at it.

Another somewhat similar but slightly smaller lizard of Australia is the bearded lizard (*Amphibolurus barbatus*). These twenty-inch bluffers can produce no frill, but have a crossways dewlap or skinfold attached to their lower jaw. When angered or frightened, the bearded lizard inflates and erects a spine-studded beard. The beard increases the lizard's apparent size. The spines, the open mouth, and more long spines on the sides of the lizard, present a fearsome sight to an enemy.

Australia also has a small desert lizard that closely resembles our American horned lizard in appearance, habits, and habitat. It is called the Moloch or thorny devil (*Moloch horridus*). Actually there is nothing horrid about it except its looks. It is an eight-inch, short-legged, short-tailed, thorny, slow-moving lizard with tan and red colors to match the desert floor. It is usually found lapping up ants, often a thousand or more a day.

Because the Australian deserts are exceptionally dry and an ant diet will not alway supply sufficient moisture, the Moloch has developed two other means of avoiding periodic dehydration. A fleshy hump near the base of the neck is loaded with stored fats acquired in times of plenty. During an extensive drought, the creature can use this fat by combining it with oxygen and chemically produce enough water to keep alive. Such chemically produced water is called metabolic water. The Moloch can also acquire a drink during a slow drizzle. Any water that falls on its skin is directed to the lizard's mouth by way of tiny grooves that wind in and out between the body scales.

84

Other desert-dwelling manufacturers of metabolic water are the mastigures or spiny-tailed lizards. Instead of having a hump, these lizards store fat in their tails. The deserts of Northern Africa, Arabia, and West Pakistan are home to several species of these two- to three-foot-long lizards. The Pakistan species of the spiny-tailed lizard is *Uromastyx hardwickii* and I once caught one just outside the desert city of Karachi. At first I thought the head sticking out of the hole in the desert floor was that of a turtle. It merely watched me approach and allowed me to gently ease its twenty-eight-inch body out. I fully expected it to bite, claw, or at least hit me with its spine-covered tail, but it remained as placid as a teddy bear.

These heavy but flat-bodied, slow-moving lizards live off the sparse vegetation around them and spend the hottest parts of the day in self-dug holes, often four feet deep. I kept my pet for several weeks, feeding it well on its natural food and releasing it back into its hole when I left Karachi.

Although many desert reptiles obtain their water by eating plants, the spiny-tailed lizards have a problem not incurred by most lizards. Due to the intense heat and lack of adequate moisture, the mastigures are adept at conserving their moisture. Like all reptiles, they lack sweat glands, but the anal glands which reclaim excess water from the urine work exceptionally well—perhaps too well. The reabsorbed water from the urine is heavy with dissolved salts acquired from eating the desert foliage, which grows in a soil having a heavy concentration of salt. In time, these salts could build up to dangerous concentrations in the lizard's body, but this problem is solved by other glands that collect surplus salts and dispose of them through the lizard's nostrils.

It is not always easy, and sometimes impossible, for a visitor in a strange country to know exactly what species of creature flashes across his vision. Therefore I shall never know for certain which lizard performed for me near the city of Bombay, India. It was dusk. The area was barren of small plants but studded with man-high shrubs. Over, between, and continually moving around the shrubs were great clouds of tiny flying insects. It was so interesting I stopped to watch. Suddenly, as one cloud neared a shrub, a small lizard leaped out and, with mouth wide open, passed directly through the mass of insects and landed with a mouthful of supper. It stayed only long enough to swallow the meal, then quickly scampered up a shrub to await another cloud. Walking through the area I saw several such lizards so engaged. Finally, I attempted to catch one, but it was dark, and the lizard reared up on its hind legs and left at top speed, dodging around shrubs and quickly disappearing. I didn't have a chance.

It could have been the variable lizard (*Calotes versicolor*) or Indian bloodsucker, as it is often known. If so, it is one of twenty-five or so members of the genus *Calotes* that ranges from India down through Burma, Sumatra, and Indonesia.

Most species of variable lizards are common enough but difficult to describe. The difficulty arises from the ease, frequency, and speed with which the *Calotes* lizards change colors. They are often called a "chameleon" because of this ability. Observers tell of watching two males battle over a female, and in the duration of one short fight, each contestant changed color several times.

These lizards average about eighteen inches long. They spend most of their time in trees and shrubs hunting insects. Eggs are laid in a hole dug in the ground. Many of their hunting grounds are right in the center of the cities within their range. They are slim, long-legged and long-tailed, and have exceptionally long flexible toes used in clasping branches and twigs. Always colorful, *Calotes* lizards are especially so when fighting or courting a female. Often their heads become a brilliant red or, in some species, a bright yellow. The red-headed species of India and Sumatra won them the name of bloodsucker.

The first wild member of the genus *Agama* that I ever saw was climbing a palm tree in South Africa. I couldn't miss it. It was about a foot long, had a bright red head, and a bluish body. In the few weeks I remained in the area, I saw many of them, but like the lizard I watched jumping through clouds of insects in Bombay, I can only guess at the species. Consulting notes and references at home, some years later, I narrowed it down to *Agama planiceps.*

Most of the fifty or so species in this genus are small, two to twelve inches in length, and most are colorful. The genus inhabits all of Africa and up into the deserts of Arabia and Iran. About the only distinguishing marks for the casual observer to notice are a somewhat flattened body and a triangular-shaped head.

Two species are best-known. One is the northern Hardun (*Agama stellio*), which is less conspicuous because of drab colors. It lives on rocky plains and deserts, but has also accepted human habitats as excellent places to hide and hunt insects or sample some of the human host's vegetables. The second is the African *Agama agama* that leads an unusually social life for a lizard. These foot-long lizards seem to establish a colony, rather than an individual territory. The colony is probably established originally by a pair which raises a family of young that remain and eventually help provide mutual protection of the area. Such lizard societies can be found throughout much of Central Africa, and strangely enough, these colony territories are usually associated with human habitats. These lizards roam the villages, spend the nights hidden in thatched roofs, and chase their insect prey down the middle of Main Street.

One of my favorite agamid lizards is the water dragon of the genus *Physignathus.* Six species of these "dragons" inhabit Australia, New Guinea, and many of the islands of Indonesia. Leseur's water dragon (*Physignathus leseurii*) of Australia so closely resembles the common iguana that the nonherpetologist has difficulty telling the difference. There is no dewlap hanging from the agamid's chin. The scales of the

Chinese water dragon

head and jowls are much smaller. The crest from the back of the head to the end of the tail is shorter, and the tail itself is shorter and stouter.

Water dragons are always associated with water. Their laterally compressed tails make a fine oar for sculling them across streams. Their nostrils are situated on top of their noses so they can lie for hours submerged, with only the tips of their noses above water to allow them to breathe. When not soaking in the water, the dragon will be soaking up sunshine on branches of overhanging trees. If frightened, it will dive into the water to escape.

We had several water dragons in our jungle at the Black Hills Reptile Gardens. The ones I liked the best were the Chinese water dragons (*Physignathus cocincinus*) of Indo-China, Cambodia, and Vietnam. The Chinese species is smaller than the Australian, only thirty inches long, but it's an all-green lizard with dark bands around its tail, and looks even more like the common iguana. They spent most of their time basking in the sun, moving with the sun from perch to perch. Often they would take time off from sunning to soak in one of the pools that dotted the area. The only real activity they engaged in was to rush down the tree or out of a pool at feeding time. To feed the many free-living lizards in the dome we set out trays of mealworms and vegetables or simply scattered crickets and mealworms generously. Our Chinese dragons were never ones to wait; they scurried right over and ate their fill. Eventually, they learned to come to me for a handout, and would accept insects directly from my fingers.

The largest and most spectacular of the agamids is the sail lizard (*Hydrosaurus amboinensis*). It is found in the Philippines and south to New Guinea. A large male may reach three and a half feet in length, and with its stout, laterally compressed tail and heavy body, it is quite impressive. It has a long, low crest of serrated scales down its back where it joins a four-inch high, crescent-shaped, skinny crest surmounting its tail. This sail-like crest consists of uninterrupted skin

Sail lizard

which is supported by extensions of bone from the tail vertebrae.

These sail-tailed lizards, as they are often called, are, like the water dragons, always found near or in the water. Being herbivores, or plant eaters, they crop the water plants and climb trees and shrubs where they eat leaves.

90

7

THE RACERUNNERS AND TEGUS

Family Teiidae

This is the speedy family. Most of its members are built for speed, with long tapering bodies, strong muscular legs, and an elongated round tapering tail. Teiids can usually be identified quickly by their velvety backs. The scales of their upper bodies are small, round, and not lapped, which give them the smooth satiny look. The lower body has rectangular plates, and on top of the head are a few large plate-like scales. Another identifying characteristic is their long, forked, snakelike tongue which they continue to run in and out to test surrounding air and ground for the smell of food or enemy. Teiids also have a bright and alert look about them at all times.

There are over 200 members in this family, most of which are native to South America. Only fifteen species live within the United States.

The few native teiids found in this country are beautiful little lizards of about ten inches to a foot in length; however, they look smaller, since much of that length is tail. Because of their speed and long whiplike tails, they are commonly called racerunners or whip-tailed lizards. Most have yellowish lines running along the sides of their brown bodies. All belong to the genus *Cnemidophorus* and, although not hard to see, they are extremely difficult to catch. They live in a condition of perpetual nervousness, moving continually, not with the graceful movements of most lizards, but with jerky starts and stops. I once sat on a boulder in a hot, dry, cactus- and rock-studded valley in Colorado watching several six-lined racerunners (*Cnemidophorus sexlineatus*) hunt for food. They scrambled over, under, and between every plant and rock within view. Their bright eyes were examining every twig, and their long tongues probed every hole or crevice. Their nervous, jerky motions finally made me nervous too, and I stood up. When I did, I realized how they earned their common name of racerunner. Every lizard within view promptly left the area at high speed. They are said to be about the fastest lizard there is. *Cnemidophorus sexlineatus* can be found throughout much of the southeastern states from Delaware south and west into Colorado.

Another species of the western whiptail (*Cnemidophorus tigris*) lives on the western side of the country, ranging from Oregon to Mexico and east to Texas. This western species can grow to be a foot long. The rest of the native whiptails are found in small areas here and there throughout the southern states and all are quite similar to the above.

There are at least two species of the genus *Cnemidophorus* that are, in one way, different from all other lizards. *Cnemidophorus tesselatus* is a fifteen-inch-long species of racerunner found in New Mexico and south into Mexico. Like all teiids, it is an egg layer but, unlike the others, almost all of its eggs hatch into females. Very few males have ever been found. Captive females, known to have never mated, produce fertile eggs. *Cnemidophorus tesselatus* is therefore called a unisexual lizard.

This ability of creatures to reproduce without the services of a male is called parthenogenesis and is carried further by the Yucatan racerunner (*Cnemidophorus cozumela*). No males of this species have ever been found, and all known hatched eggs have been female.

Ranging from Central America to southern South America are a group of several species of teiids called the jungle runners. Some of

92

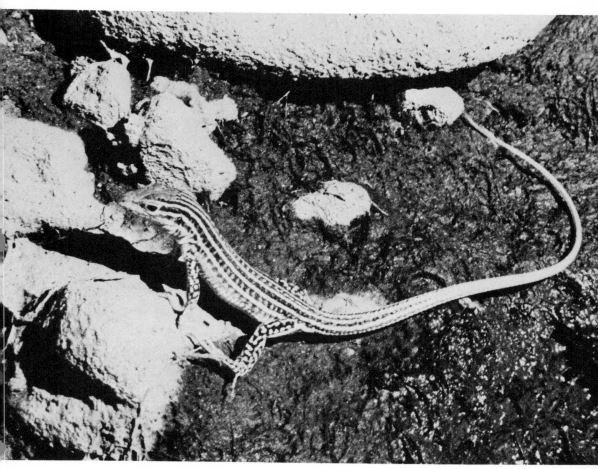

Racerunner or whiptail lizard

these are beautifully colored, extremely fast lizards of over two feet long. Jungle runners, or *Ameiva* lizards, prowl the tropical jungle floors searching for insects, spiders, or anything else they can conquer.

Ameivas are popular with reptile exhibitors because of their beauty. The colors of the Amazon jungle runner (*Ameiva ameiva*) vary but are predominantly greens, blues, and even reds. If kept warm, moist, and well fed with live insects, the jungle runners do well in captivity,

93

but need room for exercise. They are adept at dashing out of their enclosure door during servicing and quite difficult to catch again. One has to grab so fast to retrieve a loose ameiva that it's very easy to injure it. I found that a soft, small-mesh, butterfly net quickly dropped over it is the easiest and safest method. It seems inevitable that some jungle runners would escape captivity, and some did in the Miami area of Florida, and have formed the beginning of a flourishing colony.

In northeastern South America, where the Amazon River and its tributaries create thousands of miles of soft marshy soil, there lives another teiid lizard. This one can attain four feet in length and because the scales on its back resemble the back of the South American alligator or caiman, it is called the caiman lizard (*Dracaena guianensis*).

They are not often seen in zoos; they are too difficult to find or capture. When the spring floods reach the Amazon, the home soil of the caiman lizards' territory is flooded and the lizard spends much of its time in and under the water. When the water recedes, it leaves soft, mushy soil that will not support a man. The diet of a wild *Dracaena* is composed of snails and mussels. It has even developed several large, rounded crushing teeth in the back of its jaws. This is an unusual type of teeth for a lizard.

A caiman lizard dives to the bottom of the water to find and gather snails and mussels, then rises to the surface where it tips back its head to allow the hard-shelled prey to fall back between the crushing teeth. Once the shells are broken, the contents are swallowed and the shells spat out. A zoo would find it both difficult and expensive to provide sufficient snails and freshwater mussels to keep a four-foot lizard healthy. Zoos are experimenting with a more readily obtained and less expensive diet.

The most outstanding members of the Family Teiidae are called tegus, three species of which range over most of South America. Tegus

94

are, in many respects, similar to the monitor lizards. They are fast, adept hunters, and quite fierce if captured. People who farm in tegu country do not like them at all. They steal chickens, eat the eggs, are too fast to catch, and do most of their raiding at night. Some South American people hunt tegus for sport and meat. A few actually "fish" for them with a line baited with meat. The bait is dangled near, over, or often right down into the holes that tegus dig in the soil. Hungry lizards can't resist the bait, so bite and hang on as the "fisherman" pulls them in. Even then, this very capable fighter of three to four feet in length is not readily subdued.

Tegus are long, sleek-looking, shiny-scaled lizards. Like the monitors, they have powerful jaws, sharp claws, and even use their tails as

Common tegu

weapons. When fresh-caught tegus arrive at a zoo, they must be approached with respect. Some species even rear up and charge the keeper whenever possible. Within a few weeks, after learning to live on a ration of hamburger and eggs, the lizards usually quiet down, and a few become positively docile and friendly.

The gold-spotted tegu (*Tupinambis teguixin*) seems to be the most common and easiest to collect. The black-and-white-barred tegu (*Tupinambis nigropunctatus*) is common in zoos because it is the most striking-looking, and the red tegu (*Tupinambis rufescens*) seems the meanest—at least, the ones I worked with gave me the most trouble.

One odd characteristic of some tegus is their method of incubating their eggs. They have been known to tear open a termite nest and deposit the eggs inside. The termites immediately repair the hole and, in due time, the warm moist interior of the nest hatches the eggs. Even as newborns, they manage to claw their way out.

8

THE POISONOUS LIZARDS

Family Helodermatidae

There are but two known poisonous lizards in the world. One, the Gila monster (*Heloderma suspectum*), is found in the United States. The other, the Mexican beaded lizard (*Heloderma horridum*), lives in Mexico. Neither of these lizards has fangs for injecting their venom. Neither has venom that is notoriously deadly. Both, unlike snakes, have their venom glands in the lower jaw, and by means of grooved front teeth, try to hang onto their victims long enough for some venom to soak in. Although painful and resulting in considerable swelling, bites rarely cause death.

The Gila monster is a heavy-bodied, apparently slow but deceptively fast lizard of Arizona, with a slight invasion of the margins of adjacent states. It could be called a beautiful lizard. It grows to about two feet in length, has short legs, and a short, fat tail. This tail can be an indication of its condition because accumulated fats are stored here. A fat tail indicates a well-fed, healthy lizard; a scrawny tail means the lizard needs help. It lives on the stored fat during food shortages.

Its body is covered with lumpy, beaded scales, with slivers of bone under each scale which gives it a hard, solid feeling when picked up. It is a basic black or dark brown color, with streaks, bars, and dots of red or pink scattered generously over the body.

Over a period of many years this lizard has been collected for exhibition and study, or even by people who wished one for a pet. As a

Gila monster

result, the Gila has become scarce and is now under rigid protection. Strangely enough, although fierce and dangerous when found on the desert, the Gila becomes docile and even gentle in captivity. Even more strange is the fact that if a gentle Gila monster is taken from its exhibit cage and placed outside in the warm sun for a few hours, it nor-

Mexican beaded lizard

mally reverts to its original fierce nature. Returned to its cage, it again gradually resumes its docile disposition.

In the wild, the Gila eats young mice, birds, and bird eggs. It has little beady eyes with which it probably cannot see too well, but its long, fleshy tongue locates the nests of birds or mice. Captive Gilas dine and do well on a mixture of eggs and hamburger, which it laps up with its tongue.

The Mexican beaded lizard is a much larger lizard, having a maximum length of about three feet. Its colors run more to black and yellow. Both species are egg layers.

99

It is strongly advised that no attempts to catch wild Gila monsters or beaded lizards be practiced by amateur herpetologists. These lizards are fast, but not in running away. They habitually swing their heads and entire bodies around and make every attempt to bite. Once they do get their jaws on finger, hand, or arm, they tend to hang on despite all attempts to get them off. They have a powerful bite and a grinding motion of the jaws tears more flesh and introduces more venom.

9

THE GLASS LIZARDS
AND ALLIGATOR LIZARDS

Family Anguidae

The lizard family Anguidae is composed of an odd collection of lizards. Some of the members are normal four-legged types, while others have no front limbs and mere flaps for hind legs. There are also several species that have no legs at all. With or without legs, anguids can usually be identified by a fold of skin that forms a groove along the full body length, separating the sides and belly scales. This groove, called the lateral fold, is of the utmost importance to these lizards.

Lateral fold lizards are enclosed in tough rectangular scales that form neat rings about the body. Each scale has a large osteoderm, or bony plate, underneath, and the combination of scale and osteoderm forms an armor which not only protects them but also inhibits movement. They move with the stiff, awkward motion medieval knights must have used when wearing their armor. So inelastic is their covering that without the groove along the body they would have difficulty not only in breathing, but also in eating or carrying eggs or young. Within the fold of the lateral groove are tiny granular scales and no bony plates. This pliable portion of skin gives the lizard its only ability to expand its body for all internal functions. Aiding in identification of these lizards are the long, round, thin bodies, the tails which are often twice the length of the body, and the flicking, forked, snakelike

101

tongues. All have functional eyelids and ear openings. The family is worldwide in distribution.

It's hard to say which startles a person more, to find a snake that blinks or a lizard without legs. The genus *Ophisaurus* offers this problem and three species inhabit the United States. These lizards are commonly called the glass snakes. First, they are completely without legs. Second, their bodies are so shiny that they do look as if they were made of glass. Third, a legend has it that should you strike one, the body will shatter, and when you leave, the bits and pieces will reassemble as a whole creature.

The glass snake, or glass lizard, can quickly be distinguished from a true snake in several ways. Snakes have no eyelids or ear openings; these lizards have both functional eyelids and small round ear openings just behind the eyes. Snakes crawl with a smooth, fluid movement whereas these lizards move with obviously stiff backs. The anguids are shiny and glasslike, and snakes, although possibly smooth-scaled, could never be suspected of being molded in glass. The most definitive characteristic is the presence of the lateral fold.

The legend of the "glass snake" is preserved by any unsuspecting person who attempts to catch one. The lizard's main defense from large enemies is flight. Being stiff, the lizard is comparatively slow, so to confuse its enemy it breaks its tail off (autotomy). Because the tail of a glass lizard is at least as long as the body and breaks off close to its base, it really looks as though the lizard had been broken in half. When a new tail is grown, the original breaking point is so obvious that it could easily be believed to have been put together again.

All three species of North American glass lizards can be found in Florida. The island glass lizard (*Ophisaurus compressus*) is confined to that state. The slender or western glass lizard (*Ophisaurus attenuatus*) is found as far north as Illinois, then south to Texas, and east to Florida. The eastern glass lizard (*Ophisaurus ventralis*) inhabits the southern coastal states from the Carolinas to Louisiana. Adults measure from just under two feet to just over three feet in length. All species lay eggs.

Ranging throughout much of Europe, North Africa, and parts of Asia is another legless lizard called the slow worm (*Anguis fragilis*). It attains eighteen inches in length, of which nine inches is tail. It has about the same characteristics as the American legless species except that slow worms give birth to living young.

The largest of the glass lizards lives in eastern Europe and western Asia. It is called the sheltopusik (*Ophisaurus apodus*) and attains al-

A glass snake—sheltopusik

most four feet in length and one and a half inches in diameter. This species adds mice, birds, eggs, and whatever else it can catch to the common diet of insects. Unlike the American glass lizards, the sheltopusik has two hind legs, although they have degenerated into two useless, paddlelike appendages called vestigial legs. Vestigial means an appendage or organ that once functioned and, although still there, is no longer of any use. Like the American glass lizards, the sheltopusik is an egg layer. It also makes an excellent captive, at least one specimen having lived in captivity for close to thirty years.

All anguids are not legless. Trailing through the Rocky Mountain region of western United States, down through Texas, Mexico, and into Central and South America is another genus of Anguidae called the *Gerrhonotus* or alligator lizards. There are about twelve different species. Like the glass lizards, these also have the lateral groove, external ear openings, eyelids, and shiny scales with stiffening osteoderms and long, round tapering tails. But unlike glass lizards, alligator lizards have four stout legs. All North American alligator lizards are basically yellow-brown in color, with dark spots, blotches, or zigzag bands across the back. All seem to prefer a tree-covered, semishaded area with plentiful ground litter under which they hide and hunt.

Rather than resembling snakes, the *Gerrhonotus* more closely resembles the American alligator, hence the name, alligator lizard. Like the gator, it has four short legs which, as one wit put it, barely reach the ground. Like its namesake, the lizard drags its stomach when it walks, and as both are enclosed in tight-fitting armor which is too stiff to bend readily, both walk with an exaggerated swinging of the body from side to side. Despite their stiffness, alligator lizards are quite capable of climbing trees and shrubs. They are often found high up in pine and fir trees in search of food composed of insects, spiders, and snails. They are aided in climbing by their long prehensile tails which can bend around branches to assist in holding on.

Southern alligator lizard

The most common species are the southern *Gerrhonotus multicarinatus*, which reach about fifteen inches long, and the northern *Gerrhonotus coeruleus* of about one foot in length. The northern species extends its range from central California north to southern Canada and west to the edge of Montana. The southern species ranges from Oregon south to Mexico. Other species are found in Arizona and Texas, the eastern edge of the alligator lizards' range.

Most lay from three to thirty eggs at a time and deposit them underground to hatch. However, those females of the extreme northern

105

limitations of the range, or of the higher altitudes (10,000 or more feet), retain the eggs within their bodies until fully developed and give birth to living young.

American alligator lizards make good pets. Keeping them alive is easier than catching them complete with tails. They are all prone to drop their tails at any sign of danger. After feeding them insects or small bits of hamburger and egg for a few weeks, they become quite tame and often learn to eat from one's hand.

Others of the four-legged *Gerrhonotus* are found in Mexico, through Central America, and into the jungles of South America. Some are highly colored tree climbers that spend most of their lives high in the upper canopy of the tropical rain forests.

10

THE NIGHT LIZARDS

Family Xantusiidae

The largest of the xantusids barely reaches eight inches in length, and most of them are only three to four inches. Despite this small size, they are one of the most interesting families to science.

True to their common name of night lizards, they are seldom seen during the day, and it was not too long ago that they were considered to be rare. However, once their hiding places were known (under slabs of rocks, debris of yucca plants, or in cracks in rocks), they were found to be common enough.

At first, these lizards were thought to be geckos, as they resembled geckos with their snakelike transparent eyeshields instead of eyelids and with vertical slits for pupils. They differ by not having toe pads. Each xantusid toe ends in a claw, and instead of granular scales on the back, the xantusid has small round scales. They also have large, square scales on the underside and large platelike scales on top of the head.

Science became interested in them when it was discovered that the night lizard reproduced in a manner different from other known lizards, and somewhat like mammals. Mammals are viviparous, meaning there is a cord or tube called a placenta connecting the embryo with the mother's bloodstream. Xantusids have a primitive but functional placenta. Through this cord passes all the necessary nourishment needed for the developing young. There is no shell enclosing the embryo, just a thin embryonic sheath. Neither is there food nor liquid stored within this sheath as there is in an egg. All nourishment is provided by the blood passing through the placenta. As this is one of the main distinctions between mammals and reptiles, it demands an explanation yet to come.

The xantusids have another mammalian characteristic. Reptiles normally pay little attention to their young, whether born alive or produced by deposited eggs. Xantusids aid their young by pulling them, still within the sheath, out of their bodies. Then, using their teeth, they tear open the sheath and, by nudging or nipping the newborn, they encourage activity. Finally, the female eats the empty sheath. These are habits of many mammals, but quite unlizard-like.

Night lizards are not widely distributed. The most common and abundant is the three- to five-inch *Xantusia vigilis*, which is found in Southern California, the southern edge of Nevada, and south through western Arizona into the Baja Peninsula. Its olive-brown color allows it to blend in with the dead leaves and stalks of the prominent yucca plants and Joshua trees, in, among, or under which it hides. Two hazards of collecting them are being cut by the sharp edges of yucca stalks and leaves, or stuck on its sharp-pointed leaf ends as you sift through the dried, dead material. Grasping the lizards must also be done properly as they are prone to drop their tails.

Like all xantusids, the granite night lizard (*Xantusia henshawi*) eats any and all insects it can find. Also found in Southern California and down into the Baja Peninsula, the granite lizards received their name from the habit of living around granite rocks and ledges found throughout the area. This lizard specializes in hiding its four- to six-inch body under loose slabs of granite. To find them one must be prepared to pry, lift, and climb. It is of a light brown color with darker blotches that vary somewhat as the light, temperature, and background changes.

108

Only one other xantusid lizard lives in the United States. It is not only the largest of them all but lives in the smallest territory. The island night lizard (*Klauberina riversiana*) reaches up to eight inches in length and is found only on the California islands of San Clemente, Santa Barbara, and San Nicolas. These have been known to add a few bits of plant life to the normal insect diet.

Except for several subspecies of the already mentioned lizards, only one other xantusid exists, and it is rare indeed. It can be found only in one very small area of Cuba. The Cuban night lizard (*Cricosaura typica*) attains only three inches in length.

11

THE SKINKS

Family Scincidae

Hundreds of species of skinks can be found throughout the world. They inhabit every continent but Antarctica, and by one method or another, such as becoming isolated on a floating log, have reached and colonized most of the islands. Being heat-loving lizards, most species live in the tropical and subtropical areas, although a few specimens can be found as far north as southern Canada.

Skinks are diurnal, hunting their food while the warm sun shines and hiding during the cooler nights. Most of them are small, terrestrial or ground prowlers and can often be heard rustling through the dead leaves and twigs in search of insects to eat. Except for a few species, skinks are four-legged, long-tailed, shiny-scaled lizards that scurry off at the slightest sign of trouble. Their heads are covered with large platelike scales and their round bodies wear small, lapping scales that glisten as if varnished. Their tongues are long, flattened, fleshy organs that slide out to test for possible food.

Skinks are difficult to catch. Sharp eyes and ears can see or hear your slightest movement, and even with their short legs, they can dash into hiding in a flash. If you do manage to catch one, chances are it will bite, usually not seriously but painfully. Then it will undoubtedly drop off its tail. Their bodies have a solid feeling due to osteoderms or bony plates under each scale. Captive specimens survive well.

Several species inhabit the United States. They are usually somber-

110

Southern prairie skink

colored with light brown or yellow lines along both back and sides. Many also have blue tails and yellow or red colors on their heads. Unfortunately for those people who try to identify a species by color alone, the colors tend to change with age and during the mating season.

Most North American skinks are quite small. However, a few grow to be a foot or more long. The broad-headed skink (*Eumeces laticeps*) is one of those lizards that must be known over a period of time in order to identify it. If seen when young, it is jet black with five bright yellow stripes on its back, and the tail will be bright blue. As it grows older, the black gradually turns into brown and the yellow stripes fade away. The blue tail becomes slate-colored and the head of the male will become red. Many people call the broad-headed skink "The Scorpion," and consider them poisonous. They are not; theirs is a painful but not poisonous bite.

Unlike most skinks, this one will climb trees in search of food, but basically it remains on the ground. It is found in the southeastern quarter of the United States where the oaks, maples, and other deciduous trees grow and provide a moist and insect-filled environment.

From Nebraska through Texas and down into Mexico, there is a wide swath of states in which are found the Great Plains skink *Eumeces obsoletus*. This largest of the North American skinks reaches almost fourteen inches long. Like the broad-headed species, the Plains skink begins life as a black-bodied, blue-tailed beauty. As an adult it is just another brown skink with a yellow tinge on the lower sides. It prefers the open prairie as its home and, due to its size, adds young nesting mice or birds to the normal insect diet of skinks. The females are noted for guarding the eggs, a habit most lizards never practice.

Probably the best-known of the North American skinks is the five-lined skink (*Eumeces fasciatus*). This and its subspecies inhabit almost the entire eastern half of the United States. As with other species, only the young are easily identified by the five bright longitudinal stripes. The adults are usually all brown. Male adults will have a temporary red or orange head during the breeding season.

To see these skinks in the wild, go into some open woodland, pick a log or stump on which to sit, and wait quietly and motionless. On

112

warm sunny days when crickets chirp, grasshoppers jump, and bees and flies buzz, it's quite likely that the skinks will be out hunting. Listen for the sound of dried fallen leaves being rustled, and watch that area. The skink's brown body will not be seen as quickly as will the bright blue tail, and for this reason, many species of skinks are called simply the blue-tailed lizard.

A great variety of lesser skinks are found throughout most of the United States. They differ in size from six to nine inches in length and all are colored in various shades of brown. Most have yellow stripes and blue tails, at least when young. The number of stripes often determines their name. Besides the five-lined skink already mentioned, there is a four-lined skink (*Eumeces tetragrammus*) of Texas and Mexico, and the many-lined skink (*Eumeces multivirgatus*) of Arizona, New Mexico, and north to South Dakota. Others are the coal skink (*Eumeces anthracinus*), which will avoid danger by jumping into water and hiding below the surface; the mole skink (*Eumeces egregius*), which won its name by its unusual habit of burrowing; a western skink (*Eumeces skiltonianus*) that lives on the West Coast of the United States. The only states lacking skinks seem to be the New England states and North Dakota.

With one exception, the skinks of the United States can be recognized as skinks. The sand skink (*Neoseps reynoldsi*) of central Florida is only five inches long, and its round, snakelike body has such tiny legs that a quick look might not see them. It is light-colored, occasionally almost white, and prowls the sandy soils in search of termites and other small insects. It is best found under forest debris. It is amazing how fast this little lizard can disappear once you uncover it. Instead of using its practically useless legs, little *Neoseps* dives into the sand and, with much wriggling, disappears. If caught and examined closely, it can be seen to have eyelids, the lower one being equipped with a window. No ear openings are apparent and the lower jaw is

113

recessed into the upper—all practical equipment for sand burrowers.

Australia has a wide variety of skinks. The blue-tongued skink (*Tiligua nigrolutea*) has always been a favorite of mine, although not all Australians are fond of it. Blue-tongues are omnivorous, that is, they will eat almost anything from bananas to mice and insects to garden vegetables. When this foot-long lizard roams through Australian gardens touching and smelling everything with its flat, blue, fleshy tongue, the gardeners are appalled. When the lizard finds the vegetables to its liking and samples a bit of this or a lot of that, the Australians become angry.

Blue-tongues are gentle; at least, mine were. For years I kept one or more of the ten species and took them with me when giving lectures. Never once did any of my pets even offer to bite any member of the audience who cared to hold them. Instead, all would accept a bite of banana from one hand while being held in the other. One of

Blue-tongued skink

mine presented me with two beautiful little live-born young. They were, except for size, perfect replicas of the adults. These lizards have a gray to bluish-colored body, and the various species often have different but intricate black markings or bars on their backs. They have glossy scales, and a shorter and heavier tail than most other skinks.

Another interesting Australian skink has several common names. It is called the two-headed skink, walking pinecone, stump or bobbed-tailed, and shingle-backed lizard. Technically, it is known as *Trachydosaurus rugosus* but the common names are far more descriptive. Its scales are anything but smooth, and its tail is stunted.

The name "pinecone lizard" best describes it. Its large, rough, striated scales overlap like cedar shingles on a roof. With its short legs in motion, it does resemble a walking pinecone. The two-headed name refers to the tail, which is so stumpy and so much shaped like the head that one would hesitate to grasp it, not knowing which end will bite. Not only will it bite but it tends to hold on. An outraged or frightened stump-tailed lizard would make anyone hesitate to pick it up. When a twelve- to fourteen-inch lizard opens its mouth, the inside of which is bright red, then protrudes a beautiful blue tongue, and defies you, the contrasting colors and the size of its gape would make anyone believe the lizard to be poisonous. It is not.

The largest of all skinks lives on the Solomon Islands. The giant skink (*Corucia zebrata*) is one of the few skinks that is almost completely arboreal and vegetarian. It lives high in the trees and dines almost exclusively on the leaves. In captivity, this two-foot-long skink is quite docile in temperament and deliberate in action. It makes certain its new grip is secure before releasing hold of its present position. Its legs and toes are proportionately longer that those of its terrestrial cousins, and its toes are equipped with grasping claws. To aid in maneuvering about the treetops, it also has a long prehensile tail which winds around branches for additional support. Its pale, olive-green

Giant skink

color and slow movements help to camouflage and protect it from marauding lizard-eating birds.

No matter where you go, if the terrain and climate is suitable and comfortable for humans, one or more forms of skinks can usually be found in the vicinity. If one or two different skinks were to be collected from various areas of each continent or island, and placed collectively and simultaneously in one huge cage, even the specialist would find it difficult to determine which was which. To the casual lizard admirer, most would look and act much like the North American five-lined skink.

116

12

THE SPINY-TAILED LIZARDS

Family Cordylidae

Cordylidae is a small family of medium-sized lizards that are found only in the southern half of Africa and the island of Madagascar. Common to all species in this family is the fleshy tongue that is slightly notched at the tip and generously covered with papillae, or tiny pimplelike bumps. Another common characteristic is the presence of osteoderms or bony plates under all the head and body scales. All specimens also have well-developed holes, called femoral pores, on the underside of the hind thighs. Femoral pores are not yet understood but are suspected to have something to do with mating or marking territory with scent. Some lizards have them, some do not, and in most cases, they are difficult to find.

All across the hot, dry uplands of South Africa lives one of the better-known species of the cordylids. Once known scientifically as *Zonurus giganteus*, it has been changed to *Cordylus giganteus*. It also has several common names such as sungazer, spiny-tailed, club-tailed, or spike-tailed lizard. It is a regal-looking lizard of from twelve to eighteen inches in length, mud brown in color, and possessing a moderately long tail. The most prominent characteristic is the scales. They are hard, rough, and arranged in definite rows, ringing the back and down the sides. These regimented rows extend all the way from the back of the head to the tip of the tail. Many of the scales are keeled, and the ridge forming the keel projects out to form a triangular thorn

Sungazer or spike-tailed lizard

or spike. The last row of head scales forms a crescent of such spines, about one-half inch long in an adult, which project over the back of the neck. Shorter but equally sharp spines cover the lizard's sides and the surfaces of the well-developed legs. The tail is completely surrounded with long, sharp spines, reminiscent of some of the extinct dinosaurs. These are diurnal, ground lizards that catch and eat whatever terrestrial food they can, from insects and scorpions to mice.

To avoid enemies or merely for spending the night, sungazers either dig or appropriate abandoned holes, and some have been found living in such odd places as old termite nests. A more direct defense is to crawl into some crack or crevice in the rocks and ledges that litter the

118

area and wedge themselves in so tight that collectors claim it is practically impossible to pull them out. Their most spectacular defense is to use their spike-encrusted tail as a club. Their tails are therefore firmly attached and never broken off by self-induced measures.

These are sun lovers and have the habit of squatting on some rock or hump of soil, raising their heads and staying so for extended periods. This procedure earned them the name "sungazer."

Sungazer lizards make excellent exhibits in zoos. However, they are not good for the keepers. Handling the spike-tailed lizard can be rather tricky business. Not only do they swing their tails with speed and accuracy, but can bring their heads back in an effort to drive the head spikes into an unwary hand. Fortunately, most tame down and can be readily handled in a few months. One large female of mine once presented me with a pair of live-born young, both exactly like the female, with the one exception of red bars running down their sides. With age, the bars disappeared. A quite similar lizard of the genus *Zonosaurus* lives in Madagascar.

A less thorny edition of the sungazer lives in much the same area. By using a different type of defense, it has gained the popular name of armadillo lizard (*Cordylus cataphractus*). When threatened, like the true armadillo, it curls up to protect its vulnerable soft stomach. It actually takes the end of its tail into its mouth, and by holding on with both front teeth and its jaws, defies the enemy to get through the spines. Even should it not perform, it can be readily identified. Its nostrils, unlike those of the sungazer, project from the nose as short tubes.

The genus *Platysaurus* consists of a number of flat-bodied lizards that frequent the rocky ledges of South Africa. These foot-long lizards have long legs and granular scales and no spines. Some of the males are beautifully colored but the females are uniformly drab. To escape enemies, they, like the American chuckwalla, will jam themselves into cracks in rocky ledges where they inflate themselves with air. It is al-

119

Above: *Yellow-throated plated lizard*   Below: *Madagascan girdled lizard*

most impossible to pull them out without injury to them. Flat lizards eat insects and are very agile in catching them.

The plated lizard (*Gerrhosaurus nigrolineatus*) can grow to be two feet long. The scalation of back and sides is similar to the sungazers, with regimented rows of keeled scales encircling the body, but with no spines. Its ear opening is very apparent and the belly plates seem to have been made to fit a larger lizard; they overlap the side scales. Plated lizards are found throughout most of Central and South Africa, but only in the drier, rocky, desertlike grasslands. They are omnivorous, eating insects, plants, or whatever creatures they can catch. Both the plated and flat lizards are unusual in that they deposit their eggs in cracks and crevices of the ledges they inhabit.

Near the southern tip of Africa lives a group of nonconforming cordylids, the snake lizards of the genus *Chamaesaura*. The several members of this genus look remarkably like snakes. Although their brown bodies may reach two feet in length, two-thirds may consist of tail. They even move like snakes, gliding smoothly across the terrain without using the four tiny, practically useless legs. Slim and sleek, they normally can escape an enemy by fleeing, but should one be grasped, it normally casts off a portion of its tail. The female gives birth to living young.

13

THE TRUE LIZARDS

Family Lacertidae

The classic or true lizard, as the members of this family are often called, have no frills. All of them lack a dewlap, fringe, special adaptions, and even the ability to change color. They do have long, well-developed legs, and a long, round, tapering tail which can be dropped off if the lizard is mishandled or attacked. Lacertids are found in Europe, Asia, and Africa and, with but one exception, are egg layers. About the only special adaption in these lizards is the presence of windows in the lower eyelids of some species. The window allows them to see with their eyes closed during a sand or dust storm.

There are about 200 species, with two of them introduced into the United States. The backs and sides of these lizards are covered with small scales, some are even granular, depending on the species. The undersides are covered with rows of large scales and the tail scales are in rows that encircle it for the full length. Many of them have a throat collar of enlarged scales where the throat and body join, and others have enlarged scales just in front of the anal opening.

One of the prettier species is called the green or emerald lizard (*Lacerta viridis*). It seldom grows to be over a foot in length and is an insect eater that lives well in captivity on a diet of mealworms. Although normally all green, when the males desire to mate, they develop a bright blue color under the throat to aid in attracting a female or discouraging an antagonist.

122

The green lizards are said to be extremely territorial and practice a peculiar ritual when disputing territory boundaries. I have never seen the display, but observers say that the male will stand sideways to its adversary, arch the neck to display its blue throat, then begin to walk or mark time, but stays in one place. If the newcomer desires to fight, the two will bite and shake each other until one gives up and leaves. If one elects not to fight, it merely lowers its head to hide the blue throat, and stands still until the challenger leaves.

Green or emerald lizards are found throughout much of Europe and parts of Asia and have been introduced into the United States near Topeka, Kansas. Emerald lizards are spotty throughout their range. Being sun lovers and heat conscious, they will inhabit only those places they deem desirable. There are several other quite similar lacertids that so closely resemble the emerald lizard that only the herpetologist is qualified to separate them.

The largest species in this family and, to me, the most beautiful lizard in the world, is called the eyed or jeweled lizard (*Lacerta lepida*) and can be found from southern France to Northern Africa. It occasionally attains a length of thirty inches and is a sleek-bodied green lizard with black stippling which forms rows of circles enclosing a bright blue center.

The eyed lizard is both fast and powerful. Young ones depend chiefly on insects and worms for food, but as it grows it begins eating eggs or birds if it can catch them. It is omnivorous as an adult, eating other lizards, small mammals, and even some fruits and vegetables. My captive specimens learned to eat hamburger right from my fingers and would relish a plate of mixed hamburger and raw egg.

The *Lacerta* lizard with the greatest range and most fame is the little six-inch-long common lizard (*Lacerta vivipara*). It inhabits about all of northern Europe and Asia, from England in the west, through Europe, Russia, and Siberia east to the Pacific Ocean. Its fame comes from being the only lacertid that gives birth to living young and because it manages to live and thrive farther north than any other lizard. Some of them have been found doing well within the Arctic Circle in Norway and Sweden.

The common lizard has no special anatomy for the production of living young. It simply retains the eggs within the body until they are ready to hatch. Each embryo is enclosed in a thin cellophanelike sac that has no shell. Immediately upon issuing from the female, the young ones tear open the sacs, crawl out, and from then on they are on their own. The young are all black. As they mature they gradually assume the multishaded browns with black spots and stripes of the adult.

Another very similar-looking lizard is the sand lizard (*Lacerta agilis*). The sand lizard is slightly larger, from eight to ten inches long, and has some greenish tints on the sides. It lays its eggs in holes scooped out in the soil. The common and sand lizards are the only two lizards to be found in the British Isles. Sand lizards do not travel across Asia, but occupy about the western third of the area covered by the common lizard. Occasionally, an exceptionally large and green-sided sand lizard is thought to be one of the *Lacerta viridis*. Herpetologists can tell the difference by examining the scales; there are minute differences.

There is one more common little lizard to be found throughout southern Europe and the Mediterranean countries. It is called the wall lizard (*Lacerta muralis*). It has been mentioned in Greek and Roman literature as a common little fly-and-insect catcher that haunted the walls that surrounded cities and dwellings. They are still there and, like the green lizard, they love the bright sun and its heat, so can be seen sitting on top of walls and rocks, sunning themselves on every bright warm day. Unlike other similar lizards, they are not earthbound, but can run up and down the surface of the rocks and walls to chase flies and other insects. On cloudy days, the little ten-inch *muralis*

124

is usually crammed into some small crack or cranny trying to keep warm. Basically they are brown in color with dots of black and red on the undersides, and possibly some blue along the sides.

Another similar group of small lizards inhabits southern Europe and the islands of the Mediterranean Sea. One species (*Podarcis sicula*) has been introduced into the United States in the vicinity of New York to Pennsylvania. It is called the ruin lizard.

The *Podarcis* is so closely allied to the *Lacerta*, and the subspecies of both groups are so near alike that even herpetologists cannot always agree on identification. The southern European terrain consists of mountains, sunny valleys, grassy plains, sandy coasts, and rocky islands. These little lizards have been moving around for perhaps thousands of years, selecting a small area in which to live and staying there. In time, each little group has taken on the colors and habits best suited to its survival under its immediate conditions.

The lizards of western Asia and North Africa have more stable conditions. The many species of Lacertidae have changed just a little so that they can survive on the loose, blowing sand of these areas. Most have fringes on the toes to give them more traction and a few have developed transparent windows in their lower eyelids to act as goggles on windy days. One species (*Ophisops elegans*) has been dubbed the snake-eyed lizard because of the eyeshields. Most have long, tapering whiplike tails to act as balancing organs as they pursue insect prey across the desert.

Other lacertids have traveled to Borneo, Sumatra, and Java. Many of these have turned into tree and shrub climbers and have acquired a mixed diet—insects while on the ground and flowers and leaves when climbing. One member of the genus *Takydromus* has a tail several times longer than its body. It is said that due to a slight body, long legs, and considerable agility, it can easily run across the top of foliage and tall grasses to escape an enemy or capture insects.

14

RARE AND UNUSUAL LIZARDS

There are a few families of lizards which are either so rare, or with but three or four species that are seldom encountered, that these will all be included in this one chapter.

Family Amphisbaenidae

The Amphisbaenidae is the largest of these odd families. There are about 130 species forming this controversial group. Once it was included with the snakes, but is now associated with the lizards. Some taxonomists question whether the species are even reptiles, but at present most scientists classify them as reptiles of the suborder Lacertilia or lizard.

The name Amphisbaenidae is derived from two Greek words meaning "to walk at both ends." There are several common names such as worm lizard, worm snake, little snake with legs, or graveyard snake.

Some amphisbaenids have a long cylindrical, legless body with a loose-fitting skin and well-defined rings or ridges encircling the body. The head is flat or spade-shaped to assist in digging into and under the soil. The lower jaw is recessed into the upper. Both eyes and ears are buried under the skin, which makes the lizard look remarkably like an earthworm. The tail so nearly mimics the head that it's difficult to ascertain which is the head until the lizard thrusts out its forked tongue. Amphisbaenids have only a few but well-developed teeth.

Worm lizards are found in small selected warm areas of much of the world. They are in Africa, the Mediterranean area, South America, Mexico, and the United States. They are never plentiful and are usually found by people engaged in ground work such as grading, picking up rocks, or digging graves. The last occupation accounts for the name "graveyard snake."

Within the areas where worm lizards dwell, there are also underground homes of ants and termites. Attracted by either odor or soil vibrations, the lizards move right in with the insects. Their original intention may have been to drop in for dinner, as they eat both termites and ants, but once there, they find the warm, moist interior just right for depositing and hatching their eggs. Such insect nests are where most worm lizard eggs have been found.

One worm lizard (*Rhineura floridana*) lives in the moist sandy soils of central Florida, but looking for one would be a hopeless task. About the only time it leaves its burrow and comes to the surface is after a heavy rain, when, like the true earthworm, it must either come up or drown. Digging, however, may locate its burrow or burrows, for the worm lizard maintains a considerable underground system of holes.

With neither eyes nor ears, the worm lizard must locate its prey with its tongue and Jacobson's organs. A flicking tongue can pick up the odor of termites, ants, or beetle larvae, and the lizard crawls along the tunnel to the point of the strongest odor, then burrows right through the soil to the insect. Movements of the prey may also set up sufficient ground vibrations to guide the lizard. *Rhineura floridana* is an egg layer that grows to about one foot long.

An eight- to ten-inch worm lizard *Blanus cinereus* lives in Spain. Africa has several species, including *Monopeltis capensis*, which is the largest of these lizards, growing to sightly over two feet in length.

South America has the next largest worm lizard with the greatest range. The white-bellied worm lizard (*Amphisbaena alba*) inhabits almost two-thirds of eastern South America. These larger lizards will occasionally surface and catch and eat mice.

Another type of amphisbaenid is found in the southern half of the Baja Peninsula and one or two areas of the Mexican mainland. It is different from the other worm lizards in three ways. Its eyes are quite apparent through the thin skin covering. It produces living young and is the only amphisbaenid to do so. It has two very small and obvious front legs, and feet with five toes. It is known by the local Mexicans as the axolote and to the herpetologist as *Bipes biporus*. The axolote is about ten inches long, creamy white in color, and little-known outside its home territory or to other than herpetologists.

Family Pygopodidae

Fourteen species of snake lizards are known and some of these have been seen and recognized only once or twice. The lizards are so snake-like in appearance that even herpetologists can be fooled when only a glimpse is had of a fleeing reptile. The common name of snake lizard is appropriate. Scalefoot, another common name, is also appropriate. These lizards are apparently as devoid of limbs as a snake, but on close examination two hind appendages are found which amount to no more than small, useless scales. The snake lizards are found only in New Guinea, adjacent islands, and in Australia.

Not only are snake lizards limbless, neither do they have movable eyelids, but stare through attached, transparent shields. Furthermore, they have vertical slits for pupils, just as in many snake species. They are suspected of being closely related to geckos, and have the same soft skin and granular scales. The easiest method of telling them from

128

snakes is to look at their undersides. Snakes have long, overlapping, hard-surfaced scales running crosswise on the ventral surface. The snake lizard has the granular scales completely surrounding the body.

Snake lizards grow to lengths of six inches up to thirty inches, and their food varies with their size. Small ones, like the eight-inch *Aprasia pulchella* of Australia, probably eat insects or, being a burrowing species, worms. The two-foot *Lialis burtonis* of Australia and New Guinea is known to eat other lizards, and leads a more terrestrial life. There is much yet to be learned about the life and habits of these scalefoot lizards.

Family Xenosauridae

Only four known lizards belong to this family and little is known about any of them. They are moderate-sized lizards with mixed scalation. Hard, large scales are intermixed with granular scales. They are dull-colored, like the earth they run on, and have a double crest of heavy short scales that extend down the back to the ends of their tails. All are equipped with stout legs, and a long, tapered tail which, like a monitor lizard's tail, aids in swimming.

The Chinese crocodile lizard (*Shinisaurus crocodilurus*) of southern China does slightly resemble a small crocodile. This foot-long lizard haunts the streams and lies on the overhanging branches to sun itself. It plunges into the water to escape enemies, and possibly to feed. It is thought to eat fish, frogs, and tadpoles.

Even smaller is the *Xenosaurus rackhami* and its two similar relatives, and even less seems to be known about them. They live, well-hidden, in the tropical forests of southern Mexico and Central America. Only eight inches long and somber, earth-colored to match their jungle surroundings, they prowl the forests at night in search of nocturnal insects.

129

Family Anniellidae

Only two species of this little legless lizard have ever been found. They inhabit the west coast area of Southern California and down into the Baja Peninsula. There really isn't much to find. A large one is barely nine inches long, with a diameter of less than a lead pencil. Legless lizards, as they are commonly called, are usually colored a shiny tan with a dark stripe down the middle of the back, and a thinner stripe down either side. They have small, round, overlapping smooth scales.

Legless lizards are completely without even a hint of legs, and no indication of any ear opening. They do, however, have two eyes with movable pupils and eyelids. Being a burrowing creature that comes to the suface only when there is an adequate cover of leaves and debris, they have a lower jaw recessed into the upper to shape its head like a spade for easier burrowing. Both species give birth to one to four living young. *Anniella pulchra* is usually lighter in color than its subspecies *Anniella pulchra pulchra*, which is sometimes almost black.

15

THE TUATARA

The three-eyed lizard or tuatara (*Sphenodon punctatus*) is technically not a lizard. However, it looks like a lizard, is commonly called a lizard, and to all but the scientist, is a lizard. Therefore I am including it.

According to science, the tuatara does not even belong to the Order Squamata, but to the ancient Order Rhynchocephalia which, with the exception of this one living species, has become extinct. It is found only on a few small islands off the coast of New Zealand. There are many differences between this archaic yet still-living creature and the modern lizard. Most differences are internal, the structure of the skull, the teeth, and the lack of copulatory organs. However, there are also many differences in habits that could be readily observed, or even heard, since the tuatara can make a noise best described as a croak.

The three-eyed lizard grows to be about two feet in length and rather resembles the common iguana, complete with a short crest of fringe along its back. It is olive-colored with one yellow spot on each scale. In the center of the top of its head there is a third eye that possesses a small lens, complete with retina and nerves. Many modern lizards also show this pineal or third eye but lack the retina and nerves. No one yet knows the full use of the eye but suspect it may have had vision in the ancestral reptiles.

The islands where the tuatara lives are cold, windy, and misty, con-

Tuatara

ditions under which the modern lizard could not live. The tuatara spends its daylight hours in holes shared with a species of mutton birds or shearwaters that use the holes for nesting. At night, when it becomes far too cold (35 to 50 degrees F.) for modern lizards, the tuatara crawls out, croaks a welcome to the world, and begins eating some of the numerous insects that are themselves living upon the guano or fecal material left by the birds. It is also said by careful observers that the lizard occasionally helps itself to an egg or two or even a nestling.

Without copulatory organs or penes, such as true lizards have, the

132

tuatara mates by a method similar to birds. The cloacas, or vents, are pressed together and the sperm transferred. Mating takes place in the New Zealand summer, around December and January. Ten or more hard-shelled eggs are normally laid in holes scooped out of the sand. It takes approximately thirteen months for the eggs to hatch and about twenty more years before the little "lizards" will reach sexual maturity. It is thought that a tuatara may live as long as a hundred years.

The islands and these scientifically valuable "lizards" are rigidly protected.

BIBLIOGRAPHY

Andrada, Javier. "Spain's Bizarre Tree Climbing Lizards." *International Wildlife,* September-October 1980.

Behler, John L. and King, F. Wayne. *Field Guide to North American Reptiles and Amphibians.* New York: Alfred A. Knopf Inc., 1979.

Bergamini, David. *The Land and Wildlife of Australia.* Life Nature Library. New York: Time Incorporated, 1964.

Bogert, Charles M. "How They Beat the Heat." *Natural History,* June 1939.

————. "Little Snake with Hands." *Natural History,* August-September 1964.

————. "The Lizard with the Frightening Frill." *Natural History,* February 1957.

Breen, John F. *Encyclopedia of Reptiles and Amphibians.* Neptune City, New Jersey: T.F.H. Publications, 1974.

Carr, Archie. *The Reptiles.* Life Nature Library. New York: Time Inc., 1963.

Colbert, Edwin H. *The Age of Reptiles.* New York: W. W. Norton and Co., Inc., 1965.

Collins, Pat. "My Komodo Dragon Circus." *Animal Kingdom,* March-April 1956.

Conant, Roger. *Field Guide to Reptiles and Amphibians.* Boston: Houghton Mifflin Company, 1971.

Ditmars, Raymond L. "The Lizards." *Bulletin,* New York Zoological Society, July-August 1928.

―――. "Reptiles of the Southwest." *Bulletin,* New York Zoological Society, March 1923.

―――. *Reptiles of North America.* Garden City, New York: Doubleday and Company, 1936.

Frisch, Otto Von. "Enigmatic Lizard." *Natural History,* October 1963.

Gans, Carl. "The Chameleon." *Natural History,* April 1967.

Goin, Coleman J. and Goin, Olive B. *Introduction to Herpetology.* San Francisco: W. H. Freeman, 1962.

Klemmer, Konrad. *Grzimek's Animal Encyclopedia.* Reptiles. Vol. 6. London: Van Nostrand Reinhold, 1975.

Leopold, A. Starker. *The Desert.* Life Nature Library. New York: Time Incorporated, 1962.

Leviton, Alan. *Reptiles and Amphibians of North America.* New York: Doubleday and Company.

Loveridge, Arthur. *Reptiles of the Pacific World.* New York: The Macmillan Company, 1945.

Matthews, Harrison L. *The British Amphibia and Reptiles.* London: Methuen and Co., 1952.

Mays, Verna. "The Giant Skink of the Solomons." *International Wildlife,* November-December 1975.

Mertens, Robert. *The World of Amphibians and Reptiles.* New York: McGraw-Hill, 1960.

Mitchell, F.J. and Lindsay, H.A. "Australian Enigma: White Dragon Lizard." *Natural History,* May 1958.

Moore, Tui De Roy. "Dragon of the Sea." *International Wildlife,* March-April 1980.

Norris, Kenneth S. "Environment and a Lizard." *Natural History,* January 1963.

————. "The Lizard That Swims in the Sand." *Natural History,* June 1951.

Oliver, James A. *North American Amphibians and Reptiles.* New York: D. Van Nostrand Company, 1955.

————. "Lizards of the Sea." *Animal Kingdom,* October 1956.

————. "Big Bluff from Australia." *Animal Kingdom,* March-April 1955.

————. "Caiman Lizard—A Reptile Rarity." *Animal Kingdom,* September 1951.

Pawley, Ray. *Geckos as Pets.* Jersey City, N.J.: T.F.H. Publications, 1966.

Ripley, S. Dillon. *The Land and Wildlife of Tropical Asia.* Life Nature Library. New York: Time Incorporated, 1964.

Romer, Alfred Sherwood. *Man and the Vertebrates.* Chicago: University of Chicago Press, 1943.

Tinker, Spencer W. *Animals of Hawaii.* Honolulu, Hawaii: Tongg Publishing Company, 1941.

Tweedie, M.W.F. "Flying Reptiles." *Animal Kingdom,* February 1956.

INDEX

140

141

142